C000297837

GLORY DAYS
Bournemouth Transport
Colin Morris
Ian Allan
60th
ANNIVERSARY
SOUTHBOURNE
TUCKTON BRIDGE
CHRISTCHURCH
21
WRU 273

Front cover:
Boldly proclaiming its 'Yellow Buses' fleetname is 1981 Leyland Fleetline FE30AGR/ Alexander No 176 (MFX 176W) pictured at The Square. At the start of the 21st Century, Yellow Buses represents one of a handful of operators still ultimately in municipal ownership.
Colin Morris collection

Title page:
A busy scene at The Square, in mid-1963, sees Sunbeam MF2B trolleybus No 273 (WRU 273) heading towards Christchurch on route No 21 being followed by Leyland PD3/1 No 147 (YLJ 147). It is curious to note that the bus, delivered in 1959, was only one year newer than the 1958-built trolleybus, although the latter was destined to have a much shorter operational life.
Barry S. Watson

Contents

For Jo and Brian Millar
Met in Bournemouth some years ago

First published 2002

ISBN 0 7110 2877 X

All rights reserved. No part of this book may be reproduced or transmitted in any form or by any means, electronic or mechanical, including photocopying, recording or by any information storage and retrieval system, without permission from the Publisher in writing.

© Colin Morris 2002

Published by Ian Allan Publishing

an imprint of Ian Allan Publishing Ltd, Hersham, Surrey KT12 4RG.
Printed by Ian Allan Printing Ltd, Hersham, Surrey KT12 4RG.

Code: 0206/B1

Back cover (main picture):
For many years, Bournemouth was regarded as one of the safest of British trolleybus operators. In many ways the town, with its many hills, was ideal trolleybus country but, despite this, the network was to be converted gradually to bus operation during the 1960s. This view, taken on the last day of trolleybus operation (20 April 1969), shows the last trolleybus procession gathering outside the old swimming pool on Bournemouth Pier Approach. Today the building is as much a part of history as the trolleybuses, having been demolished and replaced by a new IMAX cinema.
Mac Cooper collection

Back cover (inset):
The Bournemouth Borough coat of arms. The motto — *Pulchritudo et Salubritas* — refers to the resort's natural beauty and the heath-restoring qualities of its climate. Hampshire roses surround the pine tree upon the coronet, although the town was transferred to Dorset in 1974. This 'full achievement' was carried upon Corporation vehicles from 1902 to 1982.
Mac Cooper collection

Introduction

The original idea of a book devoted to Bournemouth Transport in this series came from Mac Cooper, Chairman of the Aston Manor Transport Museum, Birmingham. But for other commitments, he would have written it himself. I'm sure that's been a disappointment for him, because his love of Bournemouth and its transport is patently clear for all to see. So, first and foremost, I am doubly grateful to him — for his patience, help and advice given during my visits to Birmingham and for permitting me to sift through his large collection of photographs. Choosing what not to include in the selection provided by Birmingham's 'Mr Bournemouth' has been a major task but, in his witty company, a very pleasant one.

I do believe that every book written about aspects of Bournemouth Transport over the years has included acknowledgement of the help provided by David Chalk, the recently retired Coaching Manager of the undertaking. In addition, David has himself written and designed every celebratory brochure published by Bournemouth Transport. So, I am very fortunate that he has passed his authoritative eye over my drafts and given me access to his own collection, at a time when he was assembling the official 2002 centenary booklet. In addition, he has cheerfully answered my numerous telephone calls, and I thank him warmly for his vital help.

Three senior officers of Bournemouth Transport Ltd gave of their precious time and permitted me to interview them at length. Their vigorous comments lift the text considerably towards the latter stages of this book. First, I am most grateful to Roy Edgley, Finance & Managing Director, for information given at a pleasant lunch in Cheshire — as I am also for background knowledge related to me at Christchurch by Councillor Ben Grower, Mayor of Bournemouth 2000/1, the first Secretary of the newly-formed company and currently a Council Director upon the Board. Introductions to these two gentlemen were kindly made by Ian Cunningham MBE, the first Managing Director of the company and the longest-serving top official of Bournemouth Transport, who also shared with me his fond reminiscences from a quarter of a century at the helm, recorded at Bear Wood.

My thanks also to Jim Jaye, Operations Director, and Jenny Wilkinson of Bournemouth Transport; Les Brown of the Local Taxation Department, Bournemouth; the staff of the Dorset County Record Office, Dorchester; Jan Marsh, local history specialist of Bournemouth Libraries; Classic Pictures of Christchurch; Mavis Ling of The Magpie's Nest, Northam, Southampton; and to Peter Delaney for details included in Section 1. My customary gratitude is extended to my friends Andrew Waller, Phil Davies and Alan Lambert, all of whom have made major contributions to this book and, once again, loaned me precious pictures for inclusion, as acknowledged in the captions.

As for me, I have the great good fortune to return each year to Bournemouth for a long-weekend's reunion with former students of Bournemouth College of Art, where I spent some of the happiest days of my youth — and I'm glad to say it feels just as good, even now. I have taken the opportunity to keep an affectionate eye upon Bournemouth Transport and have been known to point an occasional camera at some of its vehicles. Congratulations, Bournemouth, for keeping your splendid transport system in-house for a century. Long may that continue.

Colin Morris
Heswall, January 2002

▲ In 1950 Bournemouth Corporation took delivery of 30 Weymann-bodied Leyland PD2/3s, Nos 224-253. One of these, No 244, is pictured at the Square when relatively new. As delivered, these buses provided seating for 48, with staircases at the front and back. In the late 1950s the batch was renumbered 110-39 and rebuilt in the early 1960s with the removal of the front staircase, thus increasing the seating capacity to 58.
Ian Allan Library

▲ This 'centenary' postcard was based upon an 1805 map. The cartography is somewhat capricious in places: 'Durly' Chine is misplaced westward by a mile (that's Branksome Chine), Canford Heath and 'Wallis Down' are depicted much farther east than upon today's maps, which, incidentally, locate Bourne Bottom at the northern end of Alder Road. Nevertheless, some fascinating items are evident.
At this time, the Dorset/Hampshire boundary went along Branksome Chine, as it came to be known; there was a duck-decoy pond to the south of what became The Square; 'Sand Banks' referred to the area above East Cliff. But the most important in terms of this book is that the sand and gravel tracks depicted accurately mark the locations of the Poole, Wimborne, Charminster, Christchurch and Holdenhurst roads — the basic structure for today's 'Yellow Buses' network. *Classic Pictures*

▲ The heathland to the west of what is now the Lower Pleasure Gardens and north of Christchurch Road was, until 1856, part of the Tything of Holdenhurst. Tregonwell's piece of emergent Bournemouth was thus answerable to the parish council of that village, located on the south bank of the River Stour. Down one of its shady lanes comes a two-seat gig, in the early days by far the most common form of transport for those who could afford to keep a horse. *Colin Morris collection*

1. At the Beginning

Bournemouth, founded in the 19th century, has benefited greatly from the care shown by its successive planners. The Duke of Argyll, God bless him, labelled the emergent watering-place a 'Garden City by the Southern Sea'. Disguising it lightly in *Tess of the D'Urbervilles*, Thomas Hardy described it as a 'New World in an old one . . . a Mediterranean lounging place on the English Channel'. Others have called it 'The Evergreen Valley', 'The English Riviera' and 'The Pine City' — although a city it never was.

Some seven miles of sand beach are protected from northerly winds by 100ft cliffs, and the Chines (a Hampshire word for a coastal ravine) bring cool sea breezes into town in the hottest of summers. The 'whispering pines' add to that special character which is Bournemouth's: there is something magical about the place. So, as in *Alice through the Looking Glass*, I shall 'begin at the beginning'.

It was the building of Lewis Tregonwell's house on the west bank of the Bourne in 1810 (today the Royal Exeter Hotel stands upon the site) that gave Bournemouth an excuse to celebrate its centenary (for, as it turned out, the first time) in 1910. Prior to 1810 there were just fishermen's huts on the beach and wildfowling territory in the hinterland. When stage and mail coaches began to use the main east–west gravel track, the Tapp Arms opened its doors for refreshment, later becoming Bournemouth's first post office, in the care of Joseph Bell.

Tregonwell invited friends to build villas beside his, in what was then part of the Tything of Holdenhurst — a small village to the northeast — and constructed 'Terrace Cottages' to house the gardeners. After he died in 1832, his land was administered by the Branksome Estate for several years, that in Hampshire becoming Bournemouth's 'Branksome Ward' as that estate was dispersed.

Four years after Tregonwell's death, Sir George Gervis commissioned Benjamin Ferrey — architect of several buildings in Dorchester — to design an estate to be built on the east of the Bourne stream, the two sides to be connected by a widened wooden bridge. Of Ferrey's plan, Westover Cottages were built and, in 1838, the Bath Hotel — later to become the in-town terminus of the first two omnibus services in Bournemouth. From 1845 to 1853 Decimus Burton was engaged by Gervis to make 'proposals for improvements' in his part of the Bourne valley which, until 1856, were supervised by the Christchurch Poor Law Union — not that the new inhabitants qualified for its help.

To the east of the bridge, the gravel track became 'Christchurch Road', whilst to the west, where the fishmonger, the dairyman and the baker set up shop, 'Commercial Road'. To the north, and rising at a steep 1 in 8, was a then tree-lined Richmond Hill. At its foot on the east was a Presbyterian chapel (which made way for the Empress Hotel) and on the other side a single-storey Wilts & Dorset Bank building built of hamstone brought from Somerset by horse-drawn wagons. The bank was later relocated, the original building being extended and occupied by Hankinson's Estate Offices — the backdrop for numerous postcards of tourists aboard early-20th-century coaches.

Bournemouth in 1841 was still not big enough to be mentioned in *Pigot's Directories of Hampshire*. According to Pigot, the nearest place of importance to the east of Poole was Christchurch, whence, from William Walter Humby's King's Arms Hotel, two coaches per day ran to the new Southampton terminus station, some 24 miles away. 'The Pilot' at 8.00am and 'The Emerald' at 1.30pm had passed discreetly through Bournemouth beforehand.

▲ The sand dunes to the south of Christchurch Road were part of the Christchurch Poor Law Union's territory. Here was built the Bath Hotel. Outside it, *c*1856, are tethered the four-bay horse-buses of Francis Butler (for Poole) and William W. Humby (for Christchurch Road station). Since each has a single draw-pole, it is clear that both were drawn by two horses apiece. Their absence is evidence that stabling for both proprietors was provided at the hotel — Bournemouth's first bus depot! *Colin Morris collection*

▲ On the west wing of the entrance to that version of the Pier built in 1860 stand three examples of the local development of the bath chair. The double bath chair was drawn by a pony and had seats for two plus a driver. From 1885, Bournemouth's Horse Committee allotted Class D and relegated the single-seat bath chair to category F. Latterly simply known as 'double chairs', the two at the rear have C-spring suspension, while that at the front appears to have none whatsoever. *Colin Morris collection*

Elizabeth and Ann Sydenham's booksellers, library, reading room and 'fancy repository' had been established near the beach by 1851 (later another background for charabanc-tripper postcards), when the population stood at 691. The Southampton & Dorchester Railway (1847) had gone around to the north via Ringwood and Wimborne. A spur around to Lower Hamworthy (where the station was then known as Poole) caused the first omnibus to come into Bournemouth in 1851, Francis Butler's vehicle making two journeys per day from Poole to the Bath Hotel. William Humby quickly followed suit, going from the Bath Hotel to Christchurch and Christchurch Road (Holmsley) railway station, clearly to capture some of the London traffic, and leave Butler that from the west. They do not seem to have come to blows over the matter.

The construction in 1854 of the Royal National Sanatorium, on the east bank of the Bourne, led to other benevolent institutions' being attracted to the area. The patients, particularly the ladies, wished to hire their own exclusive transport to see the sights, rather than a more expensive landau. Accordingly, the Bournemouth Bath Chair was created — a single-seat three- (if drawn by a man) or four-wheeler (if by a hand-led donkey). They quickly proliferated, as other clinics and hydropathic hotels with resident physician opened their doors to visitors in need of pampering. It would take Bournemouth many years to live down the image which this created.

Those visitors with nothing much to complain about liked the company of friends upon their travels, so 4+1-seater carriages were provided (for the basic types see page 9 of *Glory Days: Royal Blue*) by newly-established 'fly proprietors' in the town. The town — for that is what it had now become — was deemed large enough to take some responsibility for its own affairs. On 14 July 1856 the Bournemouth Improvement Commissioners received the Royal Assent to set up various committees to oversee future developments. At first their territory amounted to a one-mile radius centred upon the steps of the Belle View Hotel (where now stands the Pavilion Theatre). Of importance to this story is the Horse, Hackney Carriage & Diseases of Animals Act Committee — to supervise the purchase, maintenance, welfare and sale of horses to pull water carts 'to lay the dust', road menders' carts, goods wagons and, later, refuse collection vehicles. It also took upon itself the right to inspect and license light hackney carriages (and those who drove them) within its area, laying down regulations as to use. Gradually everyone who offered to move practically anything on wheels was drawn in, including porters who pulled two-wheeled baskets, and even the donkey-boys at The Pier (first built in 1860), whose high spirits, the Committee felt, needed curbing.

Unfortunately, Committee minutes prior to July 1876 have not survived, but it is clear that Henry Laidlaw was a Commissioner and early member of the Horse Committee. Laidlaw's importance to the development of transport in Bournemouth has been swamped somewhat by the attention which has been paid to Thomas Elliott's 'Royal Blue'. Yet Laidlaw started in business at Dalkeith Mews, Christchurch Road in 1857 — some 28 years before Elliott. At first he provided change teams for Royal Mail coaches. When they ceased with the coming of the railways he built up the largest hackney-carriage and excursion-coach business in town. By the end of the 19th century he had additional accommodation at The Royal Mews, Norwich Road; Highcliffe Mews, Poole Hill; West Station Mews; The Arcade & Burlington Mews, Boscombe — and his Dalkeith Mews had become the Royal Carriage Bazaar, Old Christchurch Road, since he was also a builder and vendor of carriages.

Laidlaw & Co Ltd was formed in August 1877 with the financial backing of numerous local dignitaries, including the Chairman of the Improvement Commissioners and the local MP. The amazing nominal capital was £30,000 in 510 shares. Yet, just two years later, this company was wound-up voluntarily. Nevertheless, in a move which raises the eyebrow, that business was transferred to a new company with exactly the same name, but with a capital of £15,000. It was incorporated, with virtually the same shareholders, in October 1880. Laidlaw & Co Ltd ('version 2') was dissolved in June 1888. It had paid the trade creditors of 'version 1' a mere 7/6 (37½p) in the pound.

Laidlaw survived this affair rather well, being the only jobmaster deemed worthy of capital letters in subsequent directories. However, he does not seem to have received a good 'local press' afterward, and it took a popular national journal to note in August 1886 that 'Laidlaw has some

▲ Eventually the Horse Committee took powers to license any vehicle which plied for hire upon the public thoroughfares. Even the two-wheeled delivery cart is propelled by a 'licensed porter'. The Class A 'Bournemouth Rover' replica stage coach was owned by John Trowbridge, at one time Chairman of the Committee. It carried 24 passengers, most of them upon the roof. Only the gig is unlicensed, its large wheels designed to cope with unmade roads. *Colin Morris collection*

ELLIOTT'S

'Royal Blue'

Coaches ::
and Chars-a-banc

Run DAILY to the NEW FOREST and other Places of Interest in the District.

Landaus, Wagonettes, and Cabs
To and from the Stations.

Horses taken in at Livery,

LESSONS given in TANDEM or FOUR-IN-HAND DRIVING.

Booking Office (where Seats can be booked in advance):

Royal Blue and Branksome Mews,
Avenue Lane, Avenue Road,
Telephone No. 262. *Bournemouth.*

▲ Thomas Elliott, whose Royal Blue carriages plied for hire in Bournemouth from October 1885 onward, formed the basis from which was developed the famous express motor-coach service of that name. By the end of the 19th century his fleet included four replica stage coaches among its strength of 25 vehicles, and he had dabbled on a small scale with fledgling stage-carriage services (see *Glory Days: Royal Blue*). *Colin Morris collection*

TRIPS! TRIPS!! TRIPS!!!

DELIGHTFUL OUTINGS.

THE "CHAR-A-BANC,"

DURING THE SUMMER MONTHS,

Weather permitting, makes daily excursions in the neighbourhood of

BOURNEMOUTH,

INCLUDING

Corfe Castle, Bindon Abbey, New Forest, Rufus' Stone, Lymington, Lyndhurst, Lulworth, Woodbury Hill, Wimborne, Christchurch, Hordle (The Shakers' Encampment), &c., &c., &c.

These trips enable Visitors to enjoy the many beauties with which the vicinity of Bournemouth is surrounded.

The Char-a-Banc is admirably appointed and driven by an experienced whip.

Seats may be secured and places reserved for any journey at the Booking Office, the Victoria Library, the Square, where the vehicle daily starts from and returns to.

The fares are extremely moderate. Box seats are One Shilling extra.

The trips are arranged weekly and advertised in the local papers, and by bills about the town.

The Char-a-Bance may be engaged privately, for terms and all further particulars apply

H. LAIDLAW, Royal Mews,

CARRIAGE MANUFACTURER & JOB MASTER.

BOOKING OFFICE, THE VICTORIA LIBRARY.

◄ Also providing omnibuses to the town's railway stations was Henry Laidlaw, whose business was up and running well before Elliott's. It was much bigger too, enabling periodic reductions in fares. Laidlaw and his family lived in accommodation at the Royal Mews, later occupied by William Wells Graham, General Manager and founder of Hants & Dorset Motor Services Ltd, together with his family. Laidlaw had also been a member of the Horse Committee. *Colin Morris collection*

Apart from 'The Char-a-banc' (Elliott's 'Chars-a-banc' was nearer the original French) and 'Excelsior', Laidlaw named his various carriages as the fancy took him. This brake, with curved omnibus-style stairs at centre rear, possibly took its name from the 1910 visitation of Halley's Comet. The 'Branksome Arms' pub on Commercial Road, like much else, got its title from the Branksome Estate, briefly established as far east as the Bourne Stream. *Classic Pictures*

very good trips, and there are plenty of places to see, and some very nice fellows up and down' — a reference to his drivers and loading crews with their ladders. Some of his vehicles bore the name 'Excelsior', but there is no connection with the present Bournemouth coach fleet of that name.

Laidlaw also ran small horse-buses between hotels, the East and West stations, The Square and the newly-established settlements at what became Southbourne (not, in fact, south of the Bourne, but it really couldn't be called 'Eastbourne') and to Westbourne. To the exclusion of Laidlaw, stage-carriage services in the area crystallised into three main companies. The first was formed in 1889 by Messrs Mate and Peter — the Bournemouth, Boscombe & Westbourne Omnibus Co Ltd. It also ran buses from Richmond Park to the top of Richmond Hill, from Richmond Park to Bournemouth Arcade, and from The Square to Winton. By 1899 it was operating a fleet of 12-seat wagonettes and 16-, 24- and 26-seat double-decked vehicles — the largest drawn by three horses abreast.

Horsey & Rolls' General Penny Omnibus Co Ltd was next on the road, in December 1890, with 26-seaters from Ashley Road to The Square via Richmond Park, and from Pokesdown to County Gates. Welsman & Hinton followed in 1898 with the Boscombe Park, Pokesdown & Southbourne Omnibus Syndicate Ltd, running 16-seat wagonettes and 26-seat double-deckers. The latter operation became a public company in January 1900, changing its name to the Southbourne, Boscombe & Bournemouth Omnibus Co Ltd.

There was keen competition along the routes, sometimes with six horses abreast racing along loose-surfaced roads. Regulation became necessary, and on 5 September 1899 Bournemouth Corporation (formed in 1890) appointed its first passenger-transport official: George Ballard became omnibus timekeeper

Bournemouth's 'bath chair' image personified: up the sand surface of the East Cliff Promenade comes one of the resort's earliest forms of private-hire vehicle. Three-wheeled and with a glass 'window' to capture the sun's rays, its invalid passenger is drawn up the slope zig-zag fashion, to ease the back-breaking work of its 'driver'. Until 1884 and the introduction of a Class D category for single bath chairs, Bournemouth Improvement Commissioners did not require those who propelled them to be licensed. *Colin Morris collection*

A charabanc, a Royal Blue replica stage coach and a brake with straight staircase are prominent in a line-up of 12 horse-drawn carriages. 'The Square' has become a roundabout, with further two- and four-horse vehicles upon its southern side by the Lower Pleasure Gardens. Not a petrol-engined vehicle is in sight, but a new era is being ushered in by one of the first electric tramcars operated by Bournemouth Corporation. *Colin Morris collection*

Henry Laidlaw was also a builder of carriages and small omnibuses, which he sold to other jobmasters as well as operating himself. This charabanc, photographed on 21 August 1915, during World War 1, is a late survivor of its type, in the service of Henry F. Beamish. By this stage most had been altered to brake configuration, with side panels, rear entrance and central gangway, achieved by 'losing' three seats. *Colin Morris collection*

at 30 shillings (£1.50) per week. By the end of October, all routes had been properly timetabled and advertised.

Ballard's appointment coincided with the introduction of a completely new form of transport — the passenger-carrying motor wagonette. Since motor cars had become popular with local physicians, the Horse Committee gave a relatively warm welcome to a handful of pioneers who proposed to operate them in the borough. First to apply — on 21 July 1899 — was Edgar Collett, of Wilton Place, Boscombe, but his MMC 10-seater was not ready for inspection. Thus the honour of running the first 'motorbus' in Bournemouth fell to the Canford Cliffs Motor Omnibus Co, which firm was granted licences to run from Bournemouth Square to County Gates (and on to Canford Cliffs). The first of its three tiller-steered MMC 6½hp 7- to 9-seaters entered service on 28 September 1899, driven by Walter Le Breton.

John S. Norman was the next to seek licences, followed closely by Messrs Pickford & Bell's Bournemouth Motors Ltd of Woodside Road, Pokesdown. Both firms started in January 1900, Norman running mainly between The Square, Wellington Road, Richmond Hill and Winton, whilst Bournemouth Motors Ltd competed against BB&W horse buses between Pokesdown and County Gates. All three firms displayed fare charts and were supervised by Ballard. Edgar Collett eventually entered service in May 1900, also covering the BB&W's main route.

Already feeling the pinch, the horse-bus companies then discovered that the Corporation was to form a Tramways & Parliamentary Committee. This, together with the attentions of the motor wagonettes, prompted winding-up procedures, although, as late as December 1906, the only vehicles licensed to work on Sundays were some privately-owned horse-buses. Meanwhile the MMCs rarely operated at a loss. The flurry of their activity was at

The first double-decker omnibus in Bournemouth was operated by Henry Beamish. He transferred that and two other buses to the newly-formed Bournemouth, Boscombe & Westbourne Omnibus Co Ltd in April 1889 and concentrated solely upon excursions and tours. BB&W added to its fleet this new three-horse bus, built at Alex Dodson's Omnibus Works and photographed prior to delivery at Harmood Grove, Chalk Farm Road, NW1. *David L. Chalk collection*

The Canford Cliffs Motor Omnibus Co Ltd introduced the town's first petrol-engined (MMC) motorbuses in September 1899. Close on its heels with similar eight-seater tiller-steered MMC wagonettes came those of Francis J. Bell — another future Chairman of the Horse Committee — from a garage in Pokesdown. His fleet survived an accidental fire started there by a dropped oil lamp, and operated from Pokesdown to The Square and on to County Gates.
Colin Morris collection

Parked on the roundabout in The Square is the first motor charabanc in Bournemouth — a Durkopp, which ran tours to Wimborne. The proprietor, Charles Pooss, placed it in service during February 1906. It attracted many enthusiastic customers, but on this occasion one charming couple look as though they might prefer to be elsewhere. That July, a second Durkopp was purchased by Pooss, who called his pioneering enterprise 'The Tourist'.
Alan Lambert collection

its height in 1901: Edgar Collett had two 9½hp models, CCMOC three 7- to 9-seaters, Bournemouth Motors Ltd nine 6hp 8-seaters and John S. Norman two 6hp 8-seaters, making a total of 16 tiller-steered wagonettes buzzing about the place that summer — each licensed as Class B by the Horse Committee, which stubbornly kept its name. The *Motor Car* journal was to report that 'on Easter Monday [1902], every car available for public service at Bournemouth was crowded throughout the day' and advised that 'those contemplating starting such services may do so with every assurance of public favour'.

But not in Bournemouth, however, where everyone knew that the roads were to be dug up in preparation for the laying of tram lines. Francis Bell had already decided to give up locally and made an unsuccessful attempt to set up in Southampton, where electric tramways had already been established. Instead, he went to live in Stanley Road, Fulham, and ran MMC wagonettes in London until ousted by heavier opposition. Bell eventually returned to Bournemouth and became a Borough Councillor — and Chairman, for many years, of that very Tramways Committee which had put him out of business.

2. Tramways

Unlike their Hampshire neighbours to the east — at Southampton, Gosport and Portsmouth — the carriage and omnibus proprietors of 19th-century Bournemouth and Poole were never inconvenienced by the construction of horse-drawn tramways on the public highway.

The feeling amongst the Councillors in Bournemouth was that roads in the town were 'too narrow for tramways', so no action in that direction was forthcoming from within. Instead, the Provincial Tramways group, which had established itself in Portsmouth as the horse-drawn Portsmouth Street Tramways during 1874 — and even earlier in Plymouth — turned its attention to the area. In an attempt to be among the first to employ electric traction, it proposed, in 1881, to construct a line from Bournemouth East station (in Holdenhurst Road) through Westbourne to Poole station. A subsidiary company, the Bournemouth, Poole & District Light Railways (Electric) Co, was formed to seek the necessary powers. However, faced by stubborn opposition from Bournemouth Council, it was obliged to abandon the attempt — and Henry Laidlaw's horse buses continued to trade unhindered, from that direction at least.

That electric tramways eventually arrived in Bournemouth was indirectly due to the drive and determination of Emile Garcke, Managing Director of the Brush Electrical Engineering Co Ltd, based in Loughborough. Not only would Brush build electric tramcars; Garcke had also set up a powerful company to run them — the British Electric Traction Co Ltd, formed in 1896.

One of BET's many successful overtures made nationwide was to obtain the support of Poole Corporation and the Branksome Urban District Council for the building of a line from Poole railway station to County Gates (Bournemouth's western boundary) via Upper Parkstone, where a depot was to be established. Powers to do so were obtained in 1899, and a subsidiary, the Poole & District Electric Traction Co, was created to operate the line on a track with a gauge of 3ft 6in — a decision which, in effect, dictated the gauge which would be used also in Bournemouth and Christchurch.

The line, which cost in excess of £64,000 to construct, did not conform with Garcke's plan to establish local generating stations to go with his tramways but, instead, purchased its power from the Bournemouth & Poole Electricity Supply Co. It began carrying fare-paying passengers on

◄ A subsidiary of the British Electric Traction group, the Poole & District Electric Traction Co Ltd opened the first tramway in the neighbourhood in April 1901. Despite the company's close connection with the tram manufacturer Brush, only six of its 17 cars were built by that firm. This five-bay example was a G. F. Milnes 46-seater, one of four which — like the Brush examples — featured this reversed stairway arrangement that severely restricted the driver's view to his left. *C. G. Roberts*

Despite having their staircases the 'sensible' way around, the seven 41-seat Dick Kerr cars were built without canopies, leaving the unfortunate driver exposed to all the elements. No 5, the first of this batch, is at the stop — indicated by a white band, marked 'cars stop here', upon the nearest standards (traction poles) — close to C. T. Snook's Longfleet Post Office. When Bournemouth built its own tramway system it copied this method of marking its tram stops for the first few years.
Dr Roy Hartwell collection

6 April 1901. Beside BET's plan to construct extensions within the Poole and Branksome areas, there was its all-important aim to push on into Bournemouth and right through into Christchurch — its intention from the very beginning. Partly because it didn't want tramways of any stripe within Bournemouth and partly because, if there just had to be such a system built in its area (which was about to be enlarged to include Winton and Moordown in the north and Pokesdown and Southbourne in the east) Bournemouth Council felt that powers should be vested in the Corporation rather than BET, it took the far-from-unanimous decision to apply for its own Tramways Act.

So it was that the town was brought reluctantly into the electric-traction era by the provisions of the Bournemouth Corporation Tramways Act 1901. The Corporation was to employ its own generating station (at Southcote Road) to supply power for traction purposes, in addition to that for street arc lighting. This was built to the design of F. W. Lacey, the Borough Engineer & Surveyor, who was consulted by the Council on the layout of the system and most matters concerning the purchase of equipment and supplies, although he later (1908) claimed that he was responsible solely for surface repairs. The Borough Electrical Engineer, Ignatius M. Bulfin, who had worked as an engineer for the Corporation since 1893, was put in charge of supplying the current, also assuming responsibility for the track and a special conduit (pron: 'condit') system which was to be employed between The Lansdowne and the top of Poole Hill (so that unsightly overhead equipment should not spoil the gracious appearance of the town centre). In respect of the track, by 1905 he had invented the 'Bulfin Lip', bolted to the outside of a rail curve to ease the passage of trams around difficult corners — and later got a pay rise, on condition that he would not charge the Council a royalty for its use.

Upon the piecemeal opening of the system, which commenced in 1902, Cecil Barber, previously Chief Assistant to the Borough Electrical Engineer and Tramways Manager of Blackburn, was appointed Traffic Manager — with responsibility for the cars, the overhead lines and everything (except the track) which affected the traffic side of the undertaking. It was an arrangement which meant that no single officer was responsible to the Corporation for the administration of the system as a whole, and that would have serious repercussions just six years later.

BET, meanwhile, claimed that the Corporation had not built a sufficient amount of its proposed system (within a two-year timespan specified in the 1901 Act), that its powers had therefore lapsed and that the company should therefore be permitted to complete and operate the tramways. With this contentious issue about to go before the House of Lords, BET instead proposed that the Corporation might like to purchase the company's tramway interests in the area at a price to be negotiated. This was an unusual concession; as noted transport historian Charles F. Klapper wrote in 1961 (*The Golden Age of Tramways*), 'in the first year of the 20th century BET had 124 miles of electric tramway running — a tribute to [Garcke's] drive, his energy and the charm with which he withstood the powerful movement toward municipalisation which swept through the country'.

Upon hearing of this radical shift, Poole Town Council rushed to defend its interests, and Dorset County Council weighed in with an objection in principle to a Hampshire town's gaining powers to operate within Dorset. Poole, with backing from Branksome, proposed that if such a sale to Bournemouth were to take place, then the latter should sell the section west of County Gates to Poole Borough, which would then lease it back to Bournemouth Corporation. Thus Bournemouth tramcars could operate through to Towngate Street, Poole, in return for an annual sum, plus interest, which, over an agreed period of 30 years, would repay Poole (and a Branksome UDC which was about to become subsumed under that borough) its original outlay and leave it the sole owner of the tramways within its boundaries. Bournemouth, somewhat alarmed by the accumulating costs of establishing both a tramway and a regularised basis upon which to run it, agreed. All that remained now (May 1903) was to determine what price should be paid BET for its interests in Poole and at Christchurch, where it had already bought land to build a depot. BET wanted £430,000; Bournemouth Corporation thought them worth £70,000 at most. The matter was about to go through a lengthy arbitration process.

Despite the difficulties, work on constructing the system within Bournemouth had gained momentum. A double-track line from The Lansdowne to Warwick Road, Pokesdown, was opened for passenger traffic on 23 July 1902. It was reached from the new depot in Southcote Road by a single line through Church Road and Palmerston Road, joining up near Boscombe Arcade. Nineteen double-deck G. F. Milnes open-top cars were made available to run it, and from the outset they set the standard for the larger class of vehicle used until the system closed in 1936: four-bay with Brill bogies (eight wheels in total) and a finish, both inside and out, of 'first-rate condition, to help retain the reputation Bournemouth already enjoys'.

Next to be opened, on 16 October 1902, was a second, overhead-powered line from a point near the Fire Station (at The Lansdowne) in Holdenhurst Road as far as Springbourne, where it turned right into Ashley Road and joined up with the first route to the east of Boscombe Arcade. This line was reached from the depot by another single-access track along Southcote Road, joining Holdenhurst Road just to the south of the Central station bridge. The location of Southcote Road depot, beside the goods sidings of the down-graded Bournemouth East railway station, enabled the easy delivery by rail of coal for the power station, and of each new batch of tramcars — in sections, of course.

The major task in hand at this time was that imposed upon the department by the Council's conclusion about 'no unsightly overhead lines being permitted in the centre of town'. A deputation had visited Continental cities which employed the conduit system, and decided to adopt it. Electric current was fed into conductor rails buried beneath the roadway in a barrel whose base was some 3ft below the surface. This current reached the motors of the trams additionally equipped to use it (the Peckham trucked four-wheelers and all of the Brill 22E-bogied cars delivered 1902-6) by means of a 'plough' suspended on a bar beneath each tram. On the Bournemouth system this plough

◄ Its traction trolley-arm tethered, G. F. Milnes car No 7 stands in The Square at the foot of Commercial Road. This is one of the sections where power was taken from a conduit rail in the roadway. Its position between the two running rails was limited to junctions, like this one, or places where a transfer to overhead power was made. Otherwise the conduit rail moved across to form part of one of the running rails — in this case, immediately beyond tram No 7. *David L. Chalk collection*

The first of Bournemouth's lines to open was that between The Lansdowne and Warwick Road, Pokesdown. After 12 October 1902 it was possible for a tram to make the return journey via Ashley Road and the Central station, as the destination of G. F. Milnes bogie car No 4 indicates. What looks like car 13 is following. Both are at the Royal Arcade, Christchurch Road, Boscombe, in 1903. This stop was to become the terminus for Bournemouth's first motor-omnibus service. *Colin Morris collection*

At a time when the horse-drawn era was still in full swing — hackney carriages to the north of the roundabout, the larger excursion vehicles to the south — G. F. Milnes car No 20 goes westward to County Gates. There's not a traction pole to be seen in The Square, and, in front of this car, the conduit has returned to a running rail. No 40, in the background, was one of the smaller, three-bay cars, primarily intended for what became known as the 'side routes'. *Colin Morris collection*

Variously known as 'The Mayor's Car', 'The Parlour Car', 'The Wedding Car' and other grand titles to describe its original functions, car No 1 was unique upon the local tramways — it was Bournemouth's only passenger-carrying single-decker tram. It has paused in The Square whilst upon a reserved duty, taking customers to J. J. Allen's annual sale. Behind the leading bogie is the plough carrier associated with the town centre's conduit system. The car's trip-gates and lifeguards are also visible. Because trams were on rails, they did not require registration numbers.
David L. Chalk collection

worked under a slot in the offside running rail, save at junctions (as at The Lansdowne), cross-over points (as in The Square) and at the 'plough pits' for the change to overhead working. At these places, the slot rail curved across to a central position between the running rails. This permitted the plough to be cranked up (by hand) clear of the roadway and the tram to continue on its way with its overhead trolley-pole attached to the wire. There were seven such pits on the system, which sections proved comparatively expensive to run.

Although connected to the town's drainage system, the pits could be overcome in a thunderstorm as horse manure and mud was swept into the slots, bringing the trams to a temporary standstill. The accumulated dust and sand of summer and various objects such as children's hoops and bicycle wheels had the same effect. An additional team of employees proved necessary, including plough pitmen and plough-cleaners. These men joined a growing number of inspectors, timekeepers, foremen, drivers, relief drivers, conductors, relief conductors; porters, messengers, clerks, coachbuilders, carpenters, joiners, car-painters, french-polishers, car-trimmers, turners, fitters, assistant fitters, blacksmiths, overhead linesmen, car-cleaners, sandmen (to maintain sandboxes beneath the cars to aid grip on hills and bends), oilers, greasers, fitter-drivers, stokers, engine- and boiler-cleaners at the power station, point-cleaners, track-cleaners, platelayers, pointsmen, labourers, storekeepers and watchmen — all on differing pay scales, according to age or seniority. Much new employment had been provided by the tramways.

The third line to begin operation, on 18 December 1902, was that between The Lansdowne and County Gates, which employed the conduit system from just east of The Lansdowne, through The Square as far as St Michael's Church on Poole Hill. By the end of that year, several G. F. Milnes four-wheeled cars had

A typical 'side-route' tram, No 35 — a 1902 G. F. Milnes three-bay car with Peckham four-wheeled truck — passes the Fire Station in Holdenhurst Road *en route* to Winton via St Paul's Road, Lansdowne Road and Cemetery Junction. The conductor is collecting a fare from a lone top-deck passenger as the car passes a cyclist carrying home two spare tyres for his bike. Apart from another cyclist coming the wrong way towards him, the tramlines themselves were a constant threat. *Colin Morris collection*

joined the fleet, the first of 28 such trams delivered by July 1903 (Nos 21-48) which, together with single-decker No 1, brought the total number of cars up to 48 during this period.

An overhead-line service from Bodorgan Road (at the top of Richmond Hill) commenced on 22 December 1902 via Bournemouth Cemetery, Charminster Road, Capstone Road and joining Holdenhurst Road just beyond Lincoln Avenue, Springbourne — providing connections via Ashley Road to Boscombe. On 3 January 1903 a further route (also free of conduit) opened from near the Fire Station, Holdenhurst Road, turning left south of Central station into St Paul's Road and through Lansdowne Road to Meyrick Park Crescent via Cemetery Junction (as it now became known to the Tramways Department), where a temporary office was established. Already under construction was an extension to Moordown via Winton, which opened in two stages later in the month.

With exception of the east–west Pokesdown–County Gates 'main line', much of Holdenhurst Road and the four-way Cemetery Junction layout, all routes at this stage were single-tracked with passing loops. Also single-tracked was a conduit-system line on Richmond Hill, constructed at the same time as the rest of that type, but not brought into use until two four-wheelers had been fitted with special brakes in April 1903. Two drivers and two conductors were detailed to take turns on this shuttle service, provided to link The Square with the overhead line at the top of Richmond Hill.

Until the agreement with BET had been regularised, the Corporation could do no more than plan and prepare for an eastward expansion. Although BET had set its sights upon Purewell, the Corporation decided that its terminus would be in Church Street, Christchurch — a borough in its own right. Since 1901, the boundary south of the London & South Western Railway line was the River Stour, and a decision was taken to replace an existing bridge at Tuckton with a ferro-concrete structure wide enough to take a double line of tram tracks. This cost £4,173,

◄ A trio of 1902 three-bay, four-wheelers at Cemetery Junction in 1904. The driver of No 26 waits for the conductor to re-attach the trolley pole to the wire. Should such a de-wiring take place at night, all lights aboard the car would be temporarily extinguished also. No 23 is in Wimborne Road *en route* to Winton, whilst sister car No 25 emerges from Charminster Road bound for the top of Richmond Hill — almost certainly a posed arrangement for the Portsmouth-based photographer.
Colin Morris collection

and a ½d toll for crossing it was to be imposed upon passengers (until 1942, it turned out). For what was called the 'Christchurch Extension', power would be supplied by the Bournemouth & Poole Electricity Supply Co; the Board of Trade sanctioned the borrowing of £20,000 to cover the work, repayable over a period of 30 years. Ignatius Bulfin was appointed to act as Resident Engineer for the Christchurch Tramways and to become Electrical Engineer for the whole of the extended system, whilst Cecil Barber's duties were similarly extended; both were to have their salaries raised to £400 per annum.

In the interim, the arbitrators for BET and the Corporation, having altogether disagreed about the price to be paid for (1) the Poole undertaking as a going concern, (2) the rights, powers and privileges conferred upon BET by the Christchurch Act and (3) the land near Bargates, Christchurch, as a site for the proposed BET car depot, had appointed Alfred T. Laurence KC to be their umpire. His award, published on 21 December 1904, adjudged that the Corporation should pay to BET a total of £112,000 plus costs — £108,000 for the Poole Tramway undertaking and £4,000 for the Christchurch powers — in addition to a further agreed sum of £9,850.

Since the Borough Engineer had valued the 17 Poole tramcars at £8,000 the lot, that meant that the Poole and Branksome authorities would pay £50,000 each for the fixed assets west of County Gates, which sum both applied to the Board of Trade to borrow. Arbitration aside, the actual cost to Bournemouth Corporation at the outset was £17,850. This finding Council adopted on 3 January 1905. Poole immediately set about pressing for the construction of a 'Lower Line' through Parkstone, diverging at Pottery Junction, Branksome, and, after some two miles, rejoining the original line at Poole Park. Using the powers conferred by the Poole & District Light Railway (Extension) Order 1903, Poole engaged Emile Garcke's Brush Electrical Engineering Co Ltd to build and equip the loop, for £26,167 —

With rather more celebration evident than when Poole & District's trams commenced service from the same spot four years previously, a procession of decorated Bournemouth tramcars pose with crew members and spectators in Towngate Street, Poole. The occasion marks the closing of the gap between County Gates and Westbourne, and the resulting through service from Poole to Bournemouth. The Poole-style pill-box caps of the early years are much in evidence. *David L. Chalk collection*

the services to be operated by Bournemouth's trams (eventually commencing 3 August 1906) under the same leasing arrangement. The Board of Trade sanctioned a loan of £29,063 to pay for the construction work. In April 1905 Bournemouth laid track across the gap between the systems, at Westbourne and County Gates. This permitted the transfer to Southcote Road depot of pale blue Poole cars for inspection, refurbishment or repair — and in some cases simply storage. Both cars and Poole Light Railway track were found generally to be in poor condition, and £3,000 was set aside to relay track and put in new points and crossings, as well as to add two new passing-places and lengthen others.

On 25 May 1905 the Council accepted the tender, at £6,253, for the erection of tramcar sheds at Pokesdown (a four-track depot) and at Moordown (nine tracks, including a partitioned three-track paintshop). The former was to provide car accommodation for the eastern section (rather than BET's intended Bargates location at Christchurch) and complemented the newly-acquired lease of the Upper Parkstone depot, near the westward end of the 'main line'. Moordown was intended initially as a four-wheeler car depot, its allocation including several transferred from Parkstone which were undergoing piecemeal alterations at Southcote Road for an estimated £125 per vehicle.

Through-running between Poole and Bournemouth began, with due ceremony, on 3 July 1905. Work on the line from Pokesdown to Christchurch was complete by 22 September, and it was officially opened on 17 October. Even though BET's proposed track eastward to Purewell was never constructed, there were 41 overlapping stages on this, the longest tramline on the South Coast.

Most of Poole & District's workforce was re-employed by Bournemouth Corporation, with the former's Chief Clerk and Traffic Assistant, P. H. di Marco, being appointed to a similar post at the Lansdowne Crescent office. Men living near Parkstone depot continued to divide the Sunday duties west of County Gates, but, such was the influence of the Bournemouth Free Church Council, there was for several years no Sunday running east of County Gates. It took a formally-conducted poll in January 1913 to establish such a service, 'detrimental to Christian life . . . disastrous to the interests of the Working Class; and injurious to the best interests of the town' though the Church Council deemed it to be. Torrential rain poured down on 9 February 1913 upon the first such cars, which until 1926 were permitted to run in the afternoons only.

The Traffic Manager and Major J. W. Pringle RE of the Board of Trade inspected the lines in Bournemouth and on the Poole Corporation Light Railway on 2 March 1906. Pringle recommended some alterations in speed and stop regulations, which were adopted. In that same year, 10 new Brush-built bogie cars (72-81) were added to the fleet.

The first fatal accident on the system occurred on 15 January 1908, when 'a lady passenger' jumped off a car before it had stopped. The year held much worse in store. First, on 24 April, the Tramways Committee considered a letter from Cecil Barber, Engineer and Traffic Manager, asking that his designation be altered to 'General Manager', because the duties he was actually carrying out pertained to such a title. It decided to take no action. Just seven days later, on Friday 1 May 1908, seven passengers were killed and 27 people injured in the much publicised

◄ When Bournemouth acquired the Poole cars in April 1905, they were sent in batches to Southcote Road depot to be brought up to 'Bournemouth standard'. Ex-Poole car No 3, now with Bournemouth number 57 but still in Cambridge blue and white, has had its staircase and upstairs 'decency panel' brought into line. All seven cars without canopies were found to be in need of a complete re-roofing before such extensions, and extra seating, could be attempted. *David L. Chalk collection*

There's considerable evidence to show that, at first, Bournemouth intended to keep running what it still called 'the Poole Light Railway' as an identifiable entity. Some cars were repainted in Cambridge blue after conversion to Bournemouth standard, whilst at least a couple of the Dick Kerr cars retained their blue dashes and original fleet numbers only. No 5, running through to Bournemouth, is depicted as such beside the Old Town Lamp at the junction of Towngate and High Street, Poole. *Colin Morris collection*

Heading towards Moordown on single-line track in Wimborne Road, Winton, is car No 64 — ex-Poole No 10 rebuilt to Bournemouth standard and repainted in full municipal livery. It may have been one of only three of this type to be rebuilt (following complaints about them from Winton residents), since as late as July 1909 four remained 'unrepaired' on the books. Despite the single-line track at this stage, an 'up' and a 'down' line of electrical overhead is in place, even if the car has to stretch for it. *Colin Morris collection*

◄ The line to Christchurch was opened for passenger traffic on 17 October 1905, although it was structurally complete some four weeks previously. No 54, the last of six G. F. Milnes bogie cars delivered in 1904 and in original condition, approaches the looped curve out of Bargates and into Stour Road — next stop Christchurch railway station. Apparently the car has yet to be fitted with the appropriate blinds, for a paper sticker announces its destination of Upper Parkstone. *Classic Pictures, Christchurch*

◄ It may have been one of those cars intended for the shorter 'side routes', but car No 31 (and its fellow 1902 four-wheelers) was quite capable of serving upon the 1½-hour journey between Christchurch and Poole — the longest tramway route on the South Coast. Pausing beside the Christchurch council houses in the High Street, it is watched by small boys. One of them holds a hoop, much in vogue at the time. In the centre of Bournemouth, one of those stuck in the conduit could bring the whole line to a standstill. *Classic Pictures, Christchurch*

No 18, one of the first batch of 1902 G. F. Milnes bogie cars, at the terminus loop of Church Street, Christchurch Priory. Sending a tram back in the opposite direction really was little problem. Each end of the car was a mirror image of the other. The conductor simply swung the trolley arm through 180°, whilst the driver strolled through the lower saloon to identical controls at the other end. When buses finally arrived at this terminus they had to back into Church Lane, but in 1936 trolleybuses would need quite a radical solution.
Classic Pictures, Christchurch

The considerable length of the Bournemouth bogie car is evident in this picture of a somewhat dented No 75, a Brush-built vehicle which entered service in 1907. Five of this batch were originally intended to be single-deck 'combination' cars — with an enclosed saloon upon the centre of the chassis and open toastrack-style seating at both ends behind the driver. A poor summer put an end to that notion.
Philip Davies collection

◄ At the beginning of the 20th century there was a callous interest in 'disaster postcards' — the *Titanic* and *Lusitania* among them. This one, printed in faraway Yorkshire, 'celebrated' the day when Bournemouth suffered the nation's worst tram accident. Crudely produced, it locates the derailment at 'Fairy Glen' rather than Fairlight Glen — a private house which in later years became an office for Bournemouth Corporation Transport. Sadly, the card remains a collector's item! *David L. Chalk collection*

'Fairlight Glen Tram Accident'. The braking systems of car No 72 failed one after the other after it had left the top of Poole Hill eastbound towards The Square. Travelling in excess of 25mph with power lost, the tram careered off the track on the first bend in Avenue Road, went straight on across the pavement and dropped some 20ft onto its side among trees. The only 'glory' of this sad day belongs to William Wilton, the driver, who stayed at the controls and, with fractured ribs and other serious injuries, aided as many casualties as he could. Exonerated from all blame, when recovered he worked as a conductor, then a timekeeper and finally an inspector on the system.

Major Pringle returned to investigate. He concluded a censorious report with a recommendation that 'a properly qualified General Manager [be appointed and given] control over the whole department'. The existing management 'team' resorted, at one and the same time, to a display of mutual support and self-justification. Borough Engineer F. W. Lacey, whose name appeared on the rocker panels of the trams, defended Barber's role and declared that he (Lacey) would 'be glad to be relieved from the nominal position I now hold'. Ignatius Bulfin, whose much-praised 'lip' had failed to arrest the stricken tram, protested that 'the ordinary service cars have been taken around this curve since the accident . . . at speeds varying from 8 to 16mph without any sign of derailment, the sanctioned speed being 6mph [!] . . . and not a single car has shown any tendency to leave the track', and followed that with: 'If the Council are of the opinion that they can obtain the services of a more efficient engineer at a reduced salary, I shall very reluctantly . . . place my resignation in their hands'.

For his part, Cecil Barber recommended that an experienced and unbiased tramway manager be consulted. That manager was J. B. Hamilton of Leeds City Tramways and, embarrassingly for the Council, he had also to take into account that, on 18 September 1908, car No 73 had collided with car No 3 at a loop near Tuckton Bridge. Hamilton also recommended that a general manager be appointed, and suggested that Barber, whom he found 'very clever and acute', be given the post. Instead, the Council interviewed four candidates: Barber; Frank Ayton, Chief Engineer of Ipswich Tramways; P. J. Pringle (*sic*) of Burton on Trent; and Charles William Hill, Chief Assistant and Electrical Engineer to the Birmingham Corporation Tramways Department. On 30 March 1909, by a majority of one, the last-named was appointed the first General Manager of the system at a salary of £500 rising to £700. Two weeks later, Barber

For many years, visitors wishing to reach the shoreline west and east of the Pier were obliged to use the zig-zag paths cut into 45° angle of the cliff faces. Provided with bench seats at intervals and flanked by impressive plants, these proved far from unattractive to the fit and romantically-inclined. For those less so, in 1908 the Council built a cliff lift up the face of the West Cliff and a somewhat longer one on the East Cliff. This one is the former, when new. *Andrew H. Waller collection* ▸

And this one is the East Cliff Lift — with not a plant in sight. The twin lifts are controlled from the top, with a ticket attendant below. Briefly these lifts and their operators were the responsibility of the Tramways Committee. That ceased on 15 July 1908 when they were transferred to the Beach, Cliffs & Foreshore Committee. Strictly speaking, therefore, the additional lift built at Southbourne in 1935 and the subsequent history of all three are not part of the story of Bournemouth Transport — save, perhaps, that the replacement cars were built at Mallard Road depot. *Colin Morris collection* ▸

tendered his resignation and departed immediately. Ignatius Bulfin became Chief Assistant and Electrical Engineer at his existing salary.

During his two-year spell at Bournemouth, Hill installed Bundy check-clocks at various points to regulate the timekeeping of cars and to 'do away with traffic regulators and reduce the staff of inspectors', used The Square as the terminus for Poole and Christchurch cars whenever possible 'to meet the different requirements of the two distinct sides of the system', set up a Tramway Training School for 'motormen' (as drivers now became known in Bournemouth, as elsewhere) and conductors and provided a mess-room at the Central depot, whilst encouraging employees to form various social and sporting clubs. He also took an active interest in a fledgling motorbus service (qv) hatched by Barber in 1906.

◂ Built in 1901 for the Poole & District company, this five-bay G. F. Milnes car emerges from the Southcote Road works as rebuilt in 1909. It now has a spiral staircase and the narrower Bournemouth-style 'decency panels' upstairs (to stop male drivers being distracted by lady passengers' ankles!), and the trolley-pole has been relocated centrally. What was Poole's No 2 has become Bournemouth's No 56 and the full lined-out and varnished maroon and primrose livery has been applied. *David L. Chalk collection*

By June 1910 the section run on the conduit system was costing £5,156 per annum, whereas its overhead replacement would involve some £2,000 and be cheaper to operate. Additionally, 'the present danger of carriage wheels, etc slipping down the slot would disappear and full wear could be obtained from the head of the rails'. Since much of the 'gracious' centre of Bournemouth had now become blatantly commercial, the Council agreed — if somewhat reluctantly. Overhead equipment was duly installed, and the conduit ceased to be used in May 1911.

No reason is given in the minutes for the departure of Hill. On 18 August 1911, Ignatius Bulfin, clearly forgiven his earlier threat, was appointed General Manager. For him, electric traction was the answer to all passenger transport requirements in the Bournemouth area. If motorbuses were to be provided by the Council they should simply serve as feeders where the trams did not run, and attempts to establish them by 'outsiders' should be resisted if possible. This was his basic position for the further 24 years he served until his retirement.

In 1914, 10 new bogie cars were added to the fleet, the last of which (No 92) was the first Bournemouth car to have enclosed driving platforms. Twenty additional cars (Nos 93-112) delivered in 1921 and a further 20 in 1926 (113-132), both bogie car batches by Brush, were 'vestibuled' in this manner, and several earlier cars were amended in-house after World War 1, probably as a result of union 'encouragement'.

At its greatest extent, the tramway system operated by Bournemouth Corporation comprised 21.718 miles of route and 29.44 miles of track. The Corporation owned 17.08 miles within the County Borough of Bournemouth and 5.26 within the Borough of Christchurch, and was lessee of 7.1 miles of track in the Borough of Poole. There were 131 passenger cars plus one 1903 G. F. Milnes unit equipped as a breakdown van. Not one vehicle was dispensed with until withdrawals commenced in 1934.

There's no sign of it in this photograph taken at Westbourne in 1933, but Brush car No 81 was the last delivered (in 1907) with plough-carrying equipment for conduit working. There had been no further use for it after May 1911. The car still displays its vertical ventilators above the windows, however — an identifying feature in this particular group of 10 vehicles. Following the appointment of Charles W. Hill as General Manager in March 1909, the drivers were known as 'motormen'.
M. J. O'Connor

The beginning of the end for Bournemouth's trams came with the closure of the Lower Parkstone line in January 1929. In 1928 Hants & Dorset Motor Services Ltd (ironically part-owned by BET) had been permitted to run a new series of services in the Borough of Poole (where it opened a garage) between Branksome and Wallisdown, from Poole to Newtown and Upton, and to County Gates, with two journeys per day via Lower Parkstone. This brought its buses into direct competition with the trams on that loop, where the tracks were in urgent need of replacement — always a costly business. Poole therefore obtained powers (on 3 July 1928) to close the Lower Parkstone line and entered into an agreement with Hants & Dorset for the provision of a replacement service, initially for a period of seven years (to 1935), when Bournemouth's lease of the Poole section was due to expire. Since all Bournemouth's trams were open-topped and Hants & Dorset's new double-deckers coming into service were fully-enclosed, the outcome (west of County Gates, at least) was foreseeable. Ironically it was the lessee, Bournemouth Corporation Tramways Department, which was obliged to invite tenders for removing the Lower Parkstone track.

In May 1923 the Tramways Committee considered it 'very undesirable to have any [building] on the centre plot in The Square'. The Council wanted to take advantage of the offer of Capt and Mrs Harry Barker Norton to pay for the building of wooden shelters for passengers where once stood the grass-covered roundabout — some £2,000. The Committee considered this a potential 'great source of danger', with people running across The Square. It was quite right, but the Council prevailed — and Nortons' cupola and clock (at least) survive there even now! *Colin Morris collection*

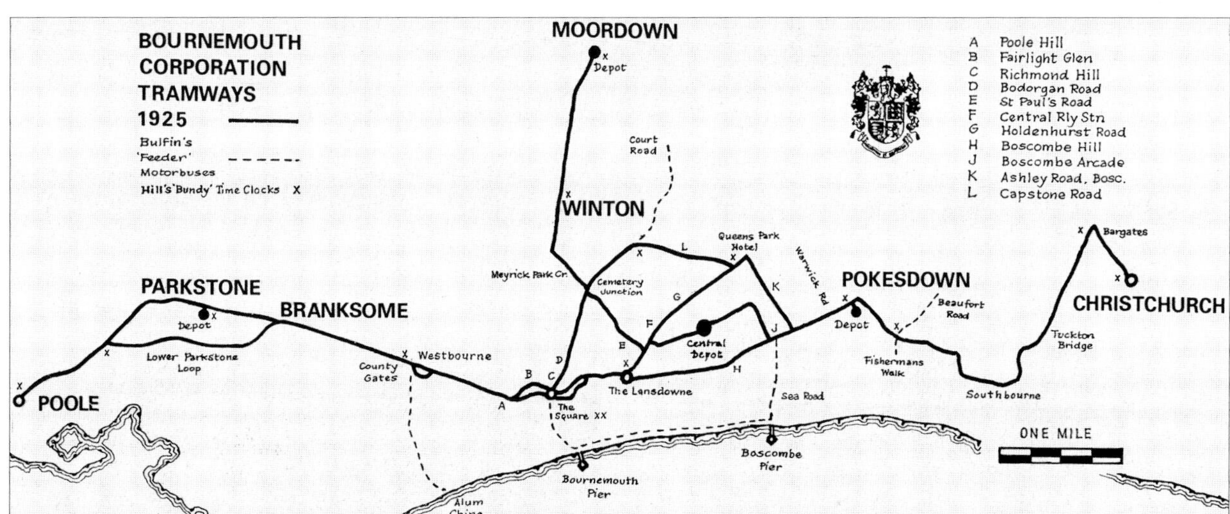

Basic map of the tram routes at their greatest extent. The line between Poole, The Lansdowne and Christchurch was always referred to by the Department as 'the Main Route'. All lines north of this were 'the Side Routes'. *Colin Morris collection*

This fine close-up picture of a 1902 three-bay, four-wheeled car would appear to have been taken at just the right time to leave us with a dilemma. The motorman wears corporal's stripes; whether this was an official badge of seniority or ex-WW1 servicemen were allowed to wear their badges of rank is not recorded in the Committee minutes. Is he one of Brig-Gen Le Marchant's 150 volunteers brought in to replace some 560 men on 'General Strike' in May 1926? He wears no medals, but 25 volunteers remained on the traffic staff in uniform to replace men 'given their cards'. *Classic Pictures, Christchurch*

As Andrew Waller points out, 'the wording on some of Bournemouth's early tram tickets seems quaint today, but throws light on the social divisions of a century ago'. All service cars running before 8am and returning between 5 and 6.30pm were available for Artisans, Mechanics and Day Labourers, but the Tramways Committee did 'not consider that young women and girls [what about the older ones?] are within that class'. Instead, a separate cheap-return ticket was issued for them, labelled 'Female Workpeoples' — a curious mixture of politically correct and incorrect, well before such things mattered so much. The tram tickets all had named stages. To avoid over-long penny tickets in the 1920s there were separate 'M' and 'S' issues, for the 'main' east–west route (Poole–Christchurch) and the 'side' routes northward. *Andrew H. Waller collection*

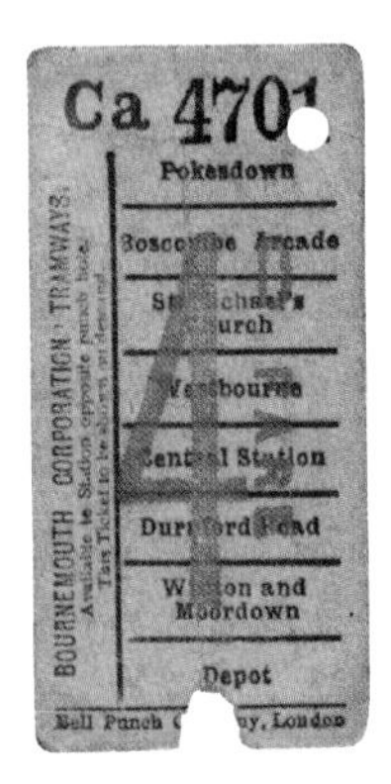

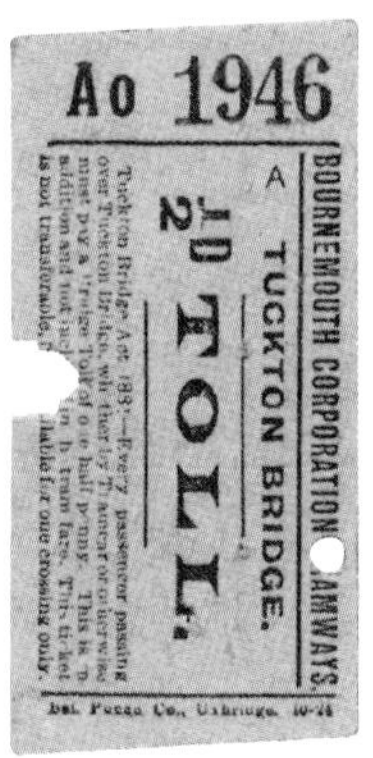

◀ Beautifully restored to its original livery at Mallard Road — a place it could not have visited during its 22 years' service in the town — is car No 85. Although constructed strictly to the standard Bournemouth pattern, the car was assembled, together with the other nine members of its batch in 1914, by the United Electric Car Co Ltd. It had been exhibited in Llandudno's green livery at the British Transport Museum, London, and returned to Bournemouth in 1974. The fleetname letters need serifs, though!
Mac Cooper collection

A traffic problem for other road users: tramtracks were laid in the middle of the road. Should one overtake a tramcar on its offside, as is the small saloon (and go into the path of oncoming traffic) or wait patiently until the tram's passengers had cleared the roadway, as is the Elliott Bros ADC coach, and go through on the inside? In the eyes of the law, the answer to that question varied over time, so one just had to keep one's eye on the local newspapers. Among motorists, at least, the tramcar was becoming a nuisance.
M. J. O'Connor

In 1914 one of 10 new tramcars delivered was fitted by its builder with vestibules at each end (glass screens to protect the 'motorman') for an extra £26 over and above the cost of £1,222 for the basic car. The rest of the batch and some earlier cars were converted later, and all subsequent new cars were vestibuled. No 108, one of the 1921 Brush cars, collects passengers in Upper Parkstone just weeks before Hants & Dorset buses took over the route. The driver of a brand-new Ford saloon plays safe and waits until the passengers board.
David L. Chalk collection

3. Trolleybuses

'Trackless Trolleys', as trolleybuses were originally known in Great Britain, were a German invention, incorporating the advantages of electric traction enjoyed by the tram, together with manœuvrability in traffic — an ability denied the tram by the predestinate grooves of its rails. They were practically silent, faster than trams and could out-accelerate a motorbus, particularly uphill. The first time that they were mentioned at a meeting of the Tramways & Parliamentary Committee was on 5 September 1910, when General Manager Charles Hill was instructed to 'keep in close touch with progress made in the development of trackless trolley systems'.

Clearly he did so, for the following month Christopher Spencer, General Manager of Bradford Tramways, wrote to say that he hoped to have his trackless trolley line in operation by the end of January 1911 and that he would be pleased to receive a deputation from Bournemouth to come and look at it. He was a good man to ask, since he had visited Germany, Austria and Italy to inspect rival trolley systems already in action. His was indeed the first system in Britain to commence operations (by half an hour over Leeds), but that start date was, eventually, 20 June 1911.

However impressed its visiting team may have been by what they saw in Bradford, it was an event upon its own doorstep which stirred Bournemouth Council into positive action. Never an easy neighbour to deal with in those days, Poole gave qualified support in 1913 to a newly-formed company — the Poole, Sandbanks & Westbourne Electric Car Co Ltd — set up to run trolleybuses along three routes not served by tramcars, but joining up with the existing system: (1) County Gates to Sandbanks via Western Road, (2) an alternative route through Ravine Road and (3) Sandbanks to Park Gates East. There were two main provisos: Board of Trade approval and the company's preparedness to sell the undertaking to Poole Borough after 15 years — so that Poole would acquire its own trolleybus system in 1929 and be in a position to extend that over its existing tramlines when Bournemouth's lease ran out. A suitably alarmed Bournemouth Council registered its opposition to such a scheme and set out to obtain Parliamentary powers to operate its own trolleybus system in conjunction with its tramways.

The re-titled Sandbanks Railless Electric Traction Co was still corresponding with Poole's Railways Committee as late as 28 August 1914. However, the outbreak of World War 1 put both attempts on hold — not surprisingly, since most of the equipment needed was now behind enemy lines — and, although Bournemouth's representatives were sent to inspect several other operators' systems in the years which followed, enthusiasm waned somewhat and, in the case of the Sandbanks company, terminally.

The first trolleybus to turn a wheel in Bournemouth was, in retrospect, a very curious vehicle. Made by Trackless Cars Ltd of Leeds, it was towed from that city for exhibition to delegates attending a Tramways & Light Railways Association Congress held in the resort during June 1922. It was an enclosed double-decker whose 'modern' bodywork looked disarmingly like a tea-cosy, and whose drive was on the front axle, which, in turn, was articulated on a primitive swivelling principle. A rather limited demonstration of its capabilities took place under tram wires at Southcote Road depot — and did not result in an order from Bournemouth.

As J. Mawson pointed out in his 1967 book *Bournemouth Corporation Transport*, the Poole Corporation Act 1928, which sanctioned closure of the Lower Parkstone tramline, also gave that borough the right to operate 'omnibuses moved by electrical power'. As he very reasonably speculates, that means that Poole seems to have been given authority to run trolleybuses some two years before Bournemouth. Most likely that was a piece of bet-hedging, should Poole decide to permit Bournemouth to replace its trams in that borough with trolleybuses when the lease came up for review in 1935. However, to the continuing benefit of Hants & Dorset, Poole was to do otherwise.

Still outwardly full of hope as far as operations west of County Gates were concerned, the Council at last secured powers to run

▲ The recently-renamed Transport Committee, having made the decision to set up an experimental trolleybus service between The Square and County Gates, selected four vehicles as demonstrators from three manufacturers. Carrying on in numerical sequence from the existing motorbus fleet, No 68 (LJ 7701) was a Sunbeam MS2 six-wheeler with 60-seat Weymann bodywork. It is parked, in later years, at Southcote Road, after conversion to standard dual staircase layout as a 52-seater. *Colin Morris collection*

With the benefit of hindsight, the two AEC contestants were an odd couple. Both based upon existing motorbus chassis, they were half-cabbed and fitted with curiously-shaped dummy radiators (this was not entirely unique, since Leyland did something similar demonstrating for other operators). No 69 (LJ 7702), an AEC 663T with English Electric 60-seat body, is in Bournemouth's two-tone primrose and maroon livery at The Square in May 1933. *Bournemouth Transport*

trolleybuses on approved tram routes on the Hampshire part of the tramway system (east of County Gates). The Bournemouth Corporation Act 1930 also authorised 14 extensions within the borough where the trams had never run. Just to be on the safe side, however, Christchurch Council succeeded in having a clause inserted which permitted it to buy 'their part' of the proposed system in 1955, or every seventh year thereafter.

Flushed with its success in Poole, and noting that Bournemouth had built up a fleet of 45 saloon motorbuses and 15 beach 'runabouts' but clearly wanted rid of its trams, in April 1931 Hants & Dorset put in a 'now or never' bid for the whole of the municipal system, which it would replace with its own motorbuses. After considerable discussion, that approach was rejected, but fears about the likely success of radical change rumbled on in committee. Reason prevailed eventually with a decision to give a thorough trial to four types of trolleybus on a properly-wired route.

In the spring of 1933, the additional two-wire overhead was attached to the existing tram-standard stretchers between The Square and Westbourne, each providing a ready-made turning loop. The four chosen vehicles, from three manufacturers, were a three-axle and a two-axle AEC, a three-axle Sunbeam and a two-axle Thornycroft. The last was the only single-decker of the quartet; Brush, its bodybuilder, did not paint its offering in Bournemouth colours, so it quickly acquired the name 'Bluebird'. After inspection by a Ministry of Transport official, the experimental service, fare 1d, started at noon on Saturday 13 May 1933, and within 10 days all four trolleybuses were at work. The novelty of this new, swift and silent service provided plenty of eager passengers, whilst the Tramways Department quickly confirmed that the promised running costs, right down to tyre wear, compared very favourably with those of motorbuses and, indeed, of the trams. The decision was taken to replace the trams with trolleybuses, and all four demonstrators were

◂ On service from County Gates to The Square whilst passing through The Triangle is No 70 (LJ 7703), the four-wheeled, 50-seat version of the AEC/English Electric combination, designated the 661T model. Both AECs were later (1934) fitted with an additional exit door, and a front staircase at the front and in 1936, their wire work complete, had their electrical equipment removed. Instead they became petrol-engined buses, serving as such until 1950. *Bournemouth Transport*

purchased in November 1933 — for £2,042, £1,853, £2,000 and £1,450 respectively.

There were two clear-cut winners as a result of the competition: the chassis manufacturer Sunbeam and the provider of the electrical equipment which came with it, British Thompson-Houston. However, instead of the Weymann coachwork fitted to the trial vehicle, the first new Sunbeam MS2s ordered for delivery in 1934 were bodied by Park Royal (Nos 72-77) and by the firm whose bodies were on the two AEC competitors, English Electric of Preston (78-83). The fleet numbers followed on not from the trams but from six AEC Regent motorbuses of 1932, plus the four acquired trolleybus demonstrators. These vehicles were joined later in 1934 by a further six Sunbeam MS2s (84-89) bodied by Park Royal to an identical design. This became the standard Bournemouth trolleybus up to World War 2 and beyond — 56-seat, six-wheeled, incorporating front and rear staircases, an entrance at the rear and an exit door, controlled by the driver, at the front. Further examples came in 1935 (90-152) and 1936 (153-173), making a total of 103 Sunbeams plus two AECs (which were converted to petrol-powered buses in 1936) and the single-deck Thornycroft, with which to replace the tramways. There had been a fleet of 131 tramcars, but the 7.1 miles of route west of County Gates had now been relinquished.

On 24 November 1934 it had been made public by the respective participants that 'Poole Corporation shall sell and the company (Hants & Dorset Motor Services Ltd) shall purchase for the sum of £75,000 the undertaking authorised by the Poole & District Light Railway Order of 1899, including the Light Railways constructed . . . and the Tram Shed and Depot owned by (Poole) Corporation'. Bournemouth still sought to run trolleybuses in Poole as late as March 1935, but it was a fleet of new Hants & Dorset buses which took over on 8 June 1935. No trolleybuses would be operated in Dorset. The tram shed in Ashley Road, Parkstone, which had housed Bournemouth trams now became

Since, when the decision was taken to run an experimental trolleybus service, Bournemouth was already operating a sizeable fleet of Thornycroft motorbuses, it was pretty certain that this Hampshire-based manufacturer would be asked to participate. It had this Brush-bodied 32-seat BD-type single-deck demonstrator (CG 4313) available in a two-tone blue and white livery — and sent it south to join the others. *Colin Morris collection*

Once in Bournemouth, the Thornycroft was re-registered LJ 7704, eventually receiving fleet number 71, but retained its blue livery throughout the trials. Not surprisingly it was dubbed 'The Bluebird' and, to the confusion of some, retained the name when it was subsequently painted yellow. Here it is on service on 15 May 1933 in the company of a bogie tramcar and a Leyland TD2 of Hants & Dorset Motor Services Ltd.
Colin Morris collection

◄ 'The Bluebird' inherited one of the problems associated with a single-deck tram running beneath double-deck-height electric overheads — only more so. The extraordinary length of its trolley-arms in repose meant that no other bus could be parked close behind it, nor could it be backed up against a wall. All four demonstrators were eventually purchased, but No 71 was the first to be sold — to South Shields Corporation Transport in 1941.
Colin Morris collection

Hants & Dorset's Parkstone depot. The company agreed to pay a large contribution to Poole toward the cost of taking up the remaining tramlines in that borough, and the replacement buses were specially purchased 'gearless' Leylands (fleet numbers prefixed 'P' for Poole) in order that ex-tramwaymen could be taught to drive them with little difficulty.

Back in Hampshire, the Bournemouth tramway routes closed one by one, but thanks to Christchurch Council, which insisted that its tram service should continue until every section could be replaced with trolleybuses, the final line to close was that between Christchurch and The Square, tramcar No 115 making the last journey to The Square on 8 April 1936.

Meanwhile, 'tramcar man' Ignatius Bulfin at last retired in September 1935, well pleased with the smooth transition to trolleybuses. Most of the members of the Transport Department had known no other General Manager than this diminutive and Chaplinesque figure with a walrus moustache, but a veritable dynamo nonetheless.

The obvious first extension of the original trolleybus route was eastward to The Lansdowne and up Holdenhurst Road, so that the vehicles could reach Southcote Road depot without trailing a sparkling 'skate' in the tramline to complete the electrical circuit, which had been the procedure during the trials. The twin wires were then carried on along the tram route through Ashley Road, Boscombe, to Christchurch Road. Primarily for football fans — said to be the best-behaved in the land — going to Dean Court, the home of Bournemouth & Boscombe Athletic FC, a short extension to Thistle Barrow Road was included (route 25 from The Square and 25A from Westbourne).

The next two services commenced on 25 March 1935, from Westbourne (24A) and The Square (24) along Christchurch Road to Iford, where a turning circle was provided and the body of tram

By the end of 1933 the decision to build a trolleybus system had been taken by the Council, tenders having gone out for overhead equipment and vehicles. Much impressed by a tour of the Wolverhampton system in late 1930, the members of the Transport Committee were already familiar with the qualities of the Sunbeam company's product produced in that town. In 1934 No 72 (AEL 400), a Sunbeam MS2 with Park Royal body became the first of Bournemouth's new trolleybuses, costing £2,135 each. *Ian Allan Library*

Whilst the trams were still running, the trolleybus overheads were wired inboard of the tram's separate wire in each direction. The trolleybus's ability to draw into the kerb and eliminate the danger to passengers posed by other traffic is well illustrated in this picture of No 107 (ALJ 981) at Trinity Church, Old Christchurch Road. In contrast, Brush tramcar No 114 of 1926 (numbered in a separate series) remains captive to the predestinate grooves of its tracks. *Colin Morris collection*

No 1 used as a waiting room. The section between Pokesdown and Iford was not previously served by trams, so a completely new overhead was required. Service 26, from The Square to Winton and Moordown, started on 7 June and gave the Sunbeams a chance to show off their power by surging up Richmond Hill with ease. Later that month, the 27 also began running to Moordown but via The Lansdowne, and on 23 August 1935 the Charminster Road tram route was replaced with service 28, which ignored Capstone Road, going on instead to the Broadway Hotel on Castle Lane, thus breaking more new ground with electrical equipment.

This, then, was the extent of the expanding trolleybus network when Duncan P. Morrison arrived from Hull Corporation Transport to take up the post of General Manager. Among his early innovations were larger destination screens giving route details and red 'honesty boxes' near the exits of the buses for the receipt of uncollected fares.

The march toward Christchurch started with the 23 to Fisherman's Walk from The Square on 21 November 1935 (and from Westbourne the following January), continuing with the 22 from The Square to Southbourne on 23 December 1935 and being completed the following April with the 21 over Tuckton Bridge. At the Church Street terminus, a finely-balanced

The standard 1930s Bournemouth trolleybus was six-wheeled; its bodywork was of wood and metal composite construction and it inherited double entrance/exits from petrol-engined 'Tramocars' first purchased by the Council in 1925. The livery adopted has been restored to No 99 (ALJ 973), now in preservation. Although devoid of lettering and numbers when photographed in July 1989, and the destination apertures are not original, reference for these items may be gained from the illustration of No 72 opposite. *D. E. Wall*

and much-photographed steel turntable for trolleybuses was installed in what had been a public-house yard; it was constructed by Sanderson Bros of Gateshead and remains in place at the time of writing (2002).

Among the many noteworthy extensions installed prior to World War 2 were the 29 to Malvern Road in April 1937 and the 30 to Wallisdown and Columbia Road in April 1939 — both from The Square, and replacing motorbuses.

When war was declared in September 1939, trolleybuses could not, like motorbuses, be dispersed around town to avoid large-scale destruction in an air attack. As in World War 1, services suffered as members of staff joined the armed forces, and, initially, ceased at sunset. The seafront became a restricted zone, the piers were severed by explosives to prevent enemy landings, and summer visitors disappeared for the duration. In 1940, 12 Sunbeams (some with their crews) were borrowed by Wolverhampton Corporation, where several remained until 1948. The London Passenger Transport Board hired another 18 between December 1940 and 1941/2, passing nine to Newcastle upon Tyne Corporation, whence some went on to Walsall, South Shields and/or the Llanelly & District Traction Co — all returning safe, if not sound, by 1945. Back in Bournemouth, spirits were lifted by the construction and opening on 22 July 1943 of a new section of trolleybus route from Iford into Christchurch via Jumpers Corner (service 20).

In 1947 the tram shelter in The Square was demolished, but the Nortons' clock survived atop a pyramid on the replacement roundabout. Another roundabout at The Lansdowne was built at the same time, both being accompanied by some considerable re-posting and re-wiring for trolleybuses.

Sadly, General Manager Duncan Morrison died in office in November 1948. As his replacement, Douglas Reakes, the Deputy General Manager and Traffic Superintendent, was promoted to the post, in which he served until February 1962. He was therefore involved in every stage of the planning (1946) and the early stages of the construction (1947-53) of the Transport Department's new headquarters at Mallard Road — on the Strouden Farm site where, in earlier times, the Corporation's horses were cared for. The outstanding feature was a 300ft x 150ft garage with no supporting pillars. The roof is carried upon cables in reinforced concrete, running through the troughs of a wavy roof, and, over the years, architects and engineers from many countries have come to look at it. In 1965 a second garage, increasing total capacity at Mallard Road up to 200 buses, was built conventionally with a single row of pillars up the centre — and cost a great deal less than the original.

Bournemouth's own electricity-generating station at Southcote Road was closed in 1955, and power for the trolleybuses was thereafter supplied from the Southern Electricity Board grid.

Since there was insufficient room at the Christchurch terminus to create a wired turning-circle for trolleybuses, another solution had to be found. It came in 1936 with the provision off Church Street (west side) of a 14-plate steel turntable. Once placed carefully upon it, the vehicle could be swung quite easily by both crew members' 'putting their backs into it'. When lined up with the exit, the brake in the foreground was applied and the trolley poles re-attached to the wires. No 97 (ALJ 971) demonstrates. *Ian Allan Library*

▲ Bournemouth in 1935 was a transport photographer's paradise, quite apart from the rich miscellany of touring coaches to be found there. If only colour photography had been as commonplace and cheap as black and white in those days! Captured finding their way past Captain Norton's waiting rooms are two vestibuled trams, two AEC Regent double-deckers and three Sunbeam trolleybuses of the Corporation and a Hants & Dorset Leyland Lion LT1 saloon. *Mac Cooper collection*

▲ This architect's projection was Jackson & Greenen of Bournemouth's design for Bournemouth Corporation Transport's completely new depot in Mallard Road, off Castle Lane. Apart from detail differences it was opened as such, piecemeal from July 1953, to house both motor and trolleybuses. A/B indicate the barrel-vault garaging with uninterrupted floor space, C the workshops, D the administrative offices, E/F the projected canteen and assembly hall, G key workers' houses, H the wash house and J the overhead equipment department. *Sydney W. Newbery / Ian Allan Library*

A Bournemouth scene of some historical significance, taken in 1957. BUT trolleybus No 222 (KLJ 356) on a Westbourne short-working takes a rest opposite a Harrington-bodied Albion coach of Charlie's Cars, a famous local firm. Shadrach ('Charlie') Pounds, the proprietor, had been a 'four-in-hand' horse-drawn-coach driver for Elliott's Royal Blue before setting up on his own account. The name 'Charlie's Cars' would cause Bournemouth Transport a problem some 30 years hence.
Mac Cooper collection

In 1958 it was decided to renumber the fleet, so No 206 (KLJ 340) became No 240, and is seen as such en route to Westbourne in Bournemouth Square. In 1963 it was one of 10 of this batch which gained 12 extra seats by the removal of the first staircase. The shade of green used for Bournemouth's traction standards at the side of the road was chosen to be unobtrusive. The 'gunfire time switch' box on the nearer is to control a street lamp atop the pole.
Mac Cooper collection

But for World War 2, there would have been further deliveries of new trolleybuses during the 'Forties. Instead, it was not until 1950 that an additional influx took place. No 207 (KLJ 341) was one of the 24 BUT 9641T vehicles, with six wheels and 56-seat Weymann bodywork, purchased. In 1954 this one was experimentally repainted with a World War 2-style dark sand matt bauxite roof, which had been Bournemouth's gesture towards camouflage upon its trolleybuses in 1940. *Ian Allan Library*

Moordown depot closed in 1953, as Mallard Road depot opened for business. This was the year that the Bell Punch 'Ultimate' ticket machine was introduced — a mechanised system which saw off the conductor's ticket rack.

Trolleybuses reached Bournemouth Pier, via Bath Road, for the first time in 1950, and a major connecting loop along Castle Lane to Iford (31 and 32) followed in October 1951, which month saw the entry into service of the 8ft-wide BUT 9641T/Weymann trolleybuses (200-223) — the largest type used on the system. It was not until 1958 that replacements for the prewar Sunbeams began to arrive — the first of 39 Sunbeam MF2B/Weymann 63/65-seaters (258-87 and 295-303) with two axles apiece (rather than the customary three) delivered by 1962. These were supplemented by seven second-hand BUT 9611T/Weymann 56-seaters from Brighton (288-294), purchased in 1959 primarily for relief working.

When Douglas Reakes retired in February 1962, his post as General Manager was awarded to Ronald Cox from Rochdale Corporation. His stay was comparatively brief, for in July 1964 he was appointed General Manager of Edinburgh Corporation Transport. In the opposite direction in 1963 had come Ian Cunningham, previously Assistant Rolling Stock

In the late 1950s the Council once again turned to its old friends in Wolverhampton and ordered a batch of trolleybuses from Sunbeam — the first since 1936. An initial 30, bodied this time by Weymann and carrying up to 63 seated passengers apiece, despite being only two-axled, began to arrive in July 1958. Although they were not originally designed for Bournemouth, their many modifications kept the town's image flying high. No 270 (WRU 270) is *en route* to Tuckton Bridge on 7 May 1961. *Alan Lambert*

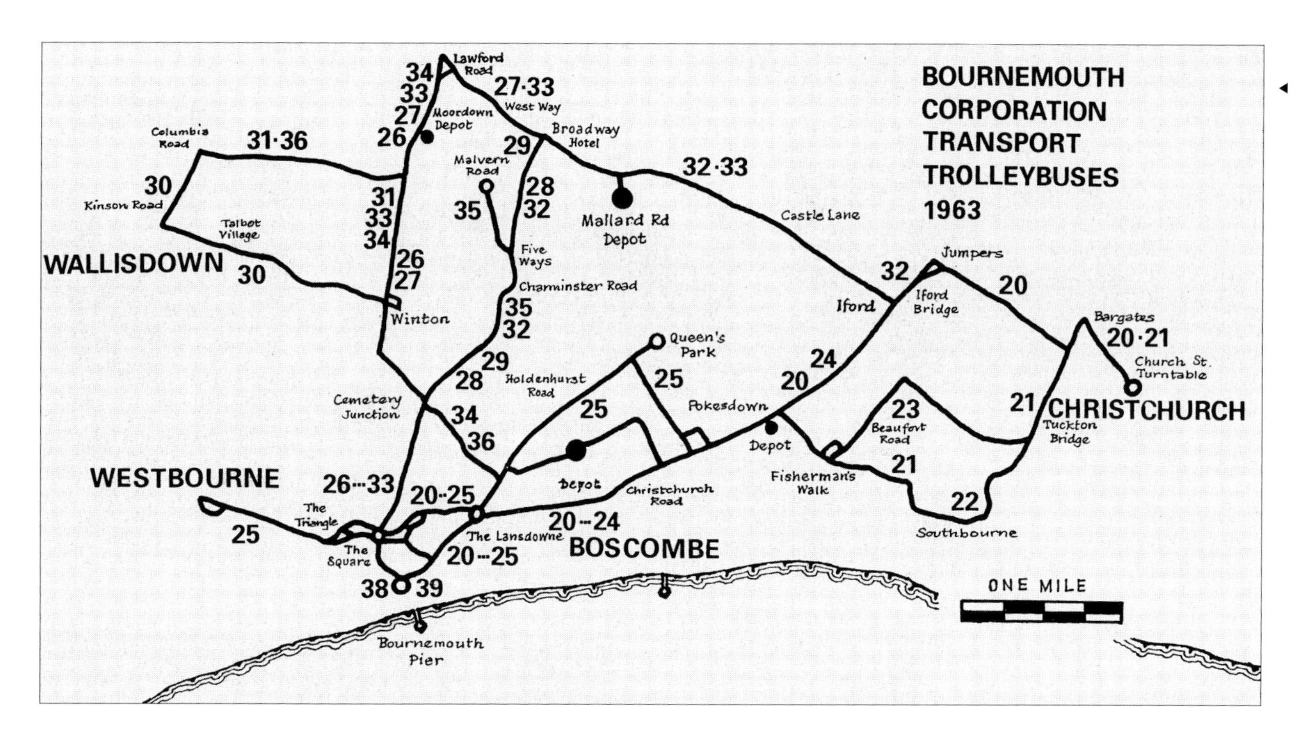

◂ Basic map of the trolleybus system at its greatest extent. Several of the original route numbers (see text) were amended in March 1956 to those shown here.
Colin Morris

Superintendent at Edinburgh, who was appointed Deputy General Manager & Engineer. Just a few months later, against stiff competition, he was appointed General Manager at Bournemouth and on course to become the undertaking's longest-serving official in that rôle.

Bournemouth Council liked its trolleybuses, and one of Ian Cunningham's early tasks was to invite tenders for some new ones — but no manufacturer was interested in quoting. 'When we pressed them, they quoted "silly figures" which were so high you couldn't consider them. We even tried to tap some foreign manufacturers, but they didn't seem interested in breaking into the British market . . . There were a whole lot of things stacked up against the trolleybus, of which the re-alignment of roads was only one. Because British firms had stopped making them, they'd also stopped making spares, and we spent a lot of time in the workshops making our own, to keep the trolleybus fleet going. The Government at the time gave to public transport operators a partial rebate of the tax upon diesel fuel, [so] we said to the electricity suppliers: "Look, you've got to reduce the price to combat this", and they said: "Well, we can't, because there's no tax on it: we can't make it any cheaper for you" . . . The construction of the town-centre bypass, Wessex Way; the underpass at the top of Richmond Hill . . . a bit here and a bit there . . . you can't run trolleybuses in a situation like that, particularly since Bournemouth's never had any battery manœuvring capability . . . Vehicle for vehicle, there was very little to choose between the running costs of a trolleybus and the replacement motorbus, but when you added the cost of maintaining the underground cables and the overhead — in other words, the electricity supply —

Recorded passing the Riverside Inn at Tuckton in the early summer of 1963, Sunbeam MF2B No 271 (WRU 271) was delivered in October 1958 and entered service in January the following year.
Barry S. Watson

Delivered in July 1969, Sunbeam MF2B No 286 (YLJ 286), seen here on the turntable at Christchurch, was destined to have a working life of less than 10 years, being withdrawn in April 1969. Initially sold to Wombwell Diesels for scrap, it was sold on to the London Trolleybus Preservation Society and today can be seen at the East Anglian Transport Museum, Carlton Colville. *M. R. Hodges*

Swinging 'Sixties — dog's-eye view: Sunbeam MF2B/Weymann trolleybus No 286 (YLJ 286) of 1959 sails through Pokesdown *en route* from Tuckton Bridge to The Square in August 1967. It is passing Warwick Road, which, in 1902, was as far east as the trams went before the construction of that bridge made possible the through journey to Christchurch. Although holding the centre of the road, the driver is doing so only because there is little other traffic. *Colin Morris*

▲ Sunbeam MF2B No 284 (YLJ 284) is pictured on Sunday 26 January 1969 negotiating the roundabout at The Square with the clock tower in the background, *en route* to Christchurch. By January 1969 the Bournemouth system was entering its last months, and No 284 was one of the vehicles to survive until the final closure, being withdrawn on 20 April 1969. *Barry S. Watson*

◄ Sunbeam MF2B No 284 (YLJ 284) is again seen on 26 January 1969, this time at Gervis Place, awaiting departure with a Christchurch service. *Barry S. Watson*

On 26 April 1958, No 160 (BRU 11), a 1936-vintage Sunbeam MS2, emerged from the new workshops with its Park Royal bodywork cut down to open-top configuration. The journey was being made for the benefit of Ministry of Transport inspectors, who noted that its front exit and staircase had been removed — thus increasing the seating capacity to 69 — and passed it fit for service. Almost immediately renumbered 201, it was one of three so treated. *G. O. P. Pearce*

Participating in an enthusiasts' tour of the system on 21 April 1969, open-topped Sunbeam No 202 (ALJ 986) — one of the celebrated three — has been turned and re-connected on the Christchurch turntable. Upon withdrawal in 1965 it had been purchased by the National Trolleybus Association, but had returned on loan to the Bournemouth Museums Department. At least six other Bournemouth trolleybuses are in preservation. *Philip Davies*

the balance was clearly in favour of the motorbus. These things all militated against the trolleybus.'

On 16 April 1963 the Council resolved 'to discontinue the use of trolley vehicles' and replace them with motorbuses. The conversions came thick and faster than envisaged. Ian Cunningham: 'When you are running down any system, there comes a point at which it is totally uneconomic to keep the rump going . . .'

In September 1963, the overhead wiring along Lansdowne Road and St Paul's Road was taken down. Unlike elsewhere, outside contractors were not used for this work. 'Our overhead maintenance gangs were all long-serving employees, so I decided to use them to take down the overhead and pull out all the underground cables. And I began to take the *Financial Times* and watched the copper prices like a hawk, and whenever the copper prices peaked at over £600 a ton, I would sell, say, half a ton of it . . . and by that means we cleared the whole of the debt on the trolleybus system.'

Southcote Road depot closed on 6 June 1965 and Pokesdown depot on 31 December 1967. The entire Bournemouth Corporation fleet was thereafter based at Mallard Road. Between September 1966 and final closure on 20 April 1969, the only trolleybus routes still running were services 20-24 along the main Christchurch Road, maintained by 29 surviving Sunbeam MF2B vehicles. Save two small-scale experiments in the 'Seventies, the 68-year era of electric traction in the area had drawn to its inevitable close.

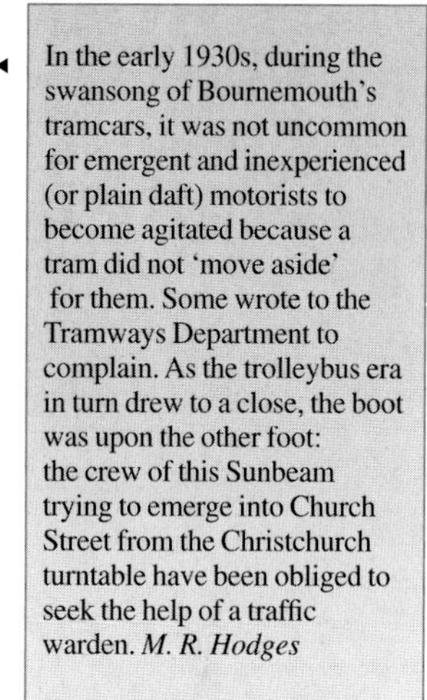

In the early 1930s, during the swansong of Bournemouth's tramcars, it was not uncommon for emergent and inexperienced (or plain daft) motorists to become agitated because a tram did not 'move aside' for them. Some wrote to the Tramways Department to complain. As the trolleybus era in turn drew to a close, the boot was upon the other foot: the crew of this Sunbeam trying to emerge into Church Street from the Christchurch turntable have been obliged to seek the help of a traffic warden. *M. R. Hodges*

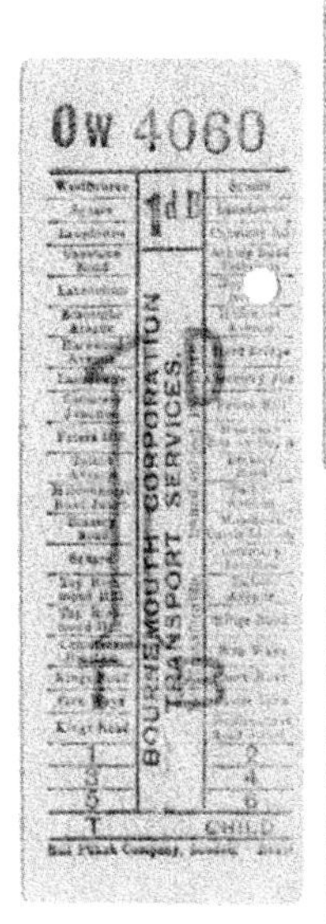
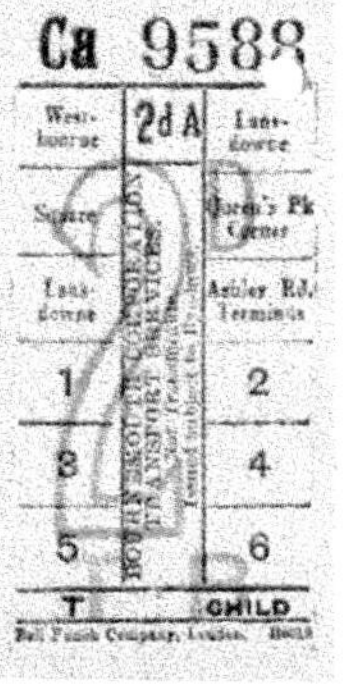
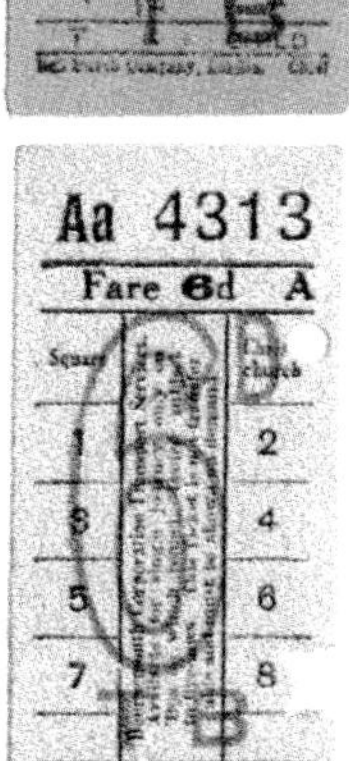
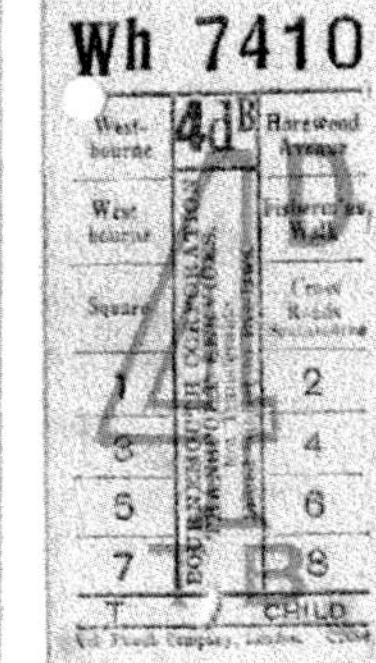
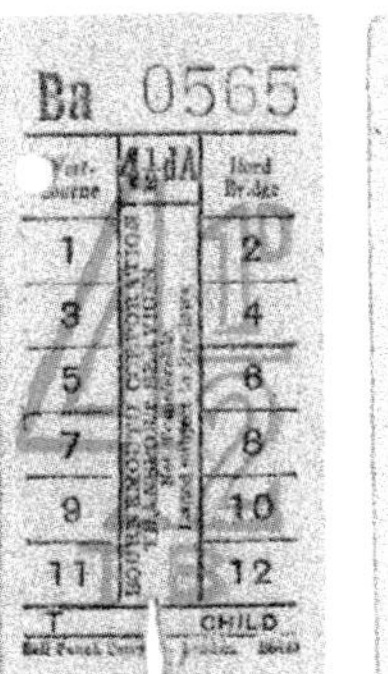
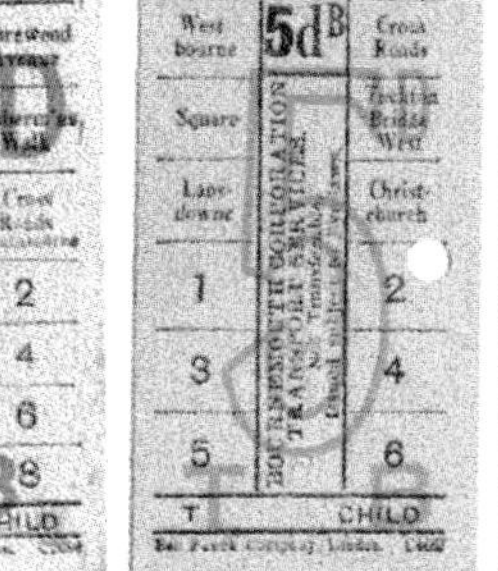

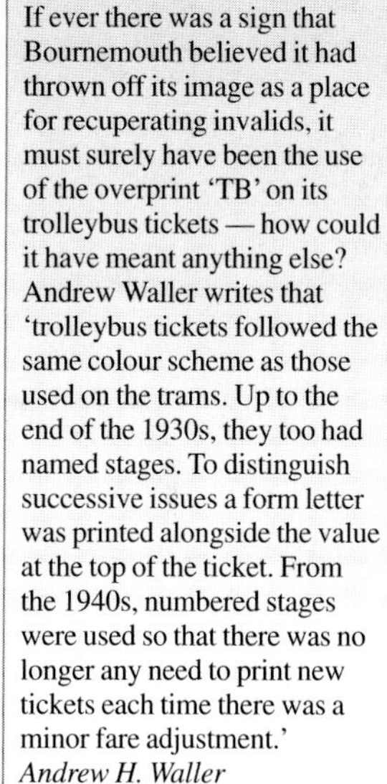

If ever there was a sign that Bournemouth believed it had thrown off its image as a place for recuperating invalids, it must surely have been the use of the overprint 'TB' on its trolleybus tickets — how could it have meant anything else? Andrew Waller writes that 'trolleybus tickets followed the same colour scheme as those used on the trams. Up to the end of the 1930s, they too had named stages. To distinguish successive issues a form letter was printed alongside the value at the top of the ticket. From the 1940s, numbered stages were used so that there was no longer any need to print new tickets each time there was a minor fare adjustment.' *Andrew H. Waller*

38
VIA
LANSDOWNE
301 LJ
301
WINTON
ENSBURY PARK
COLUMBIA ROAD
30
SCHOOL SPECIAL
297 LJ

◂◂ The final delivery of new vehicles for the Bournemouth trolleybus fleet was made in 1962. The batch comprised nine additional Sunbeam MF2B/Weymann models, this time seating 65. Nos 297 (297 LJ) and 301 (301 LJ), the last new trolleybus built for a British operator, were both acquired by the Bournemouth Passenger Transport Association after the closure of the system. That group's contribution to transport history cannot be praised enough. *Ian Allan Library*

▴ The final parade of trolleybuses, illustrated on the back cover of this book, was marshalled with particular care. The honour of being the last vehicle in the procession fell to No 301 (301 LJ), that final trolleybus built for the British market in 1962. As it hisses its way along Castle Lane to Mallard Road for the very last time, on 20 April 1969, it has on board the Mayor of Bournemouth, Alderman Michael W. Green JP. *Ian Allan Library*

◂ This excellent study of ALJ 973 (at the time No 212) in Gervis Place highlights just one of the problems which brought about the demise of British trolleybuses. They were silent, quick and powerful, giving smooth acceleration and producing no fumes and little vibration, but it was the cost of moving all that overhead equipment in road re-routing schemes which helped kill them off. The main reason, however, was that no firm seemed to want to build them anymore. *Philip Davies*

In 1959 the Corporation acquired seven trolleybuses from Brighton Corporation and Brighton, Hove & District. These Weymann-bodied BUT 9611Ts represented the only second-hand trolleybuses to operate in Bournemouth. One of the ex-BH&D vehicles, No 292 (DNJ 992), is seen at The Triangle in mid-1963 *Barry S. Watson*

Chasing a Vauxhall and a Morris around The Square in a wide arc (because that's where the wires made it easy) but heading for Richmond Hill and Columbia Road is another 1959 stop-gap purchase. One of four conventional, rear-entrance, two-axle BUT/Weymann rolleybuses acquired from Brighton Corporation, No 289 (HUF 46) was new in 1947. *Mac Cooper collection*

Photographed on 3 July 1988, at one of Mallard Road depot's popular 'open days', is part of a remarkable collection of preserved vehicles which once worked for Bournemouth Corporation Transport. No 301 (301 LJ) has become the property of the Bournemouth Passenger Transport Association, as also has AEC tower wagon VH 6217, acquired in 1945, as a double-deck bus, from Huddersfield Corporation. *D. E. Wall*

4. Corporation Motorbuses

When, at the beginning of the 20th century, the Council had prepared the legal ground for the establishment of its tramways, it had the good sense to foresee that some unscheduled interruption of services might occur. Accordingly, the Bournemouth Corporation Act 1901 had allowed for the substitution of a temporary motorbus service. The provision was extended by the 1904 Act to include trial running over proposed tramway routes to gauge the traffic potential. Since, at the time, the only motor-buses running in the borough were the privately-owned MMC wagonettes of Francis Bell and his rivals, this type of traction was not perceived by the councillors as being of much greater use.

It was a letter dated 22 April 1905 from the Rev H. Ebben, chairman of the Bournemouth East Interests Association, which focused Council minds somewhat. A resolution had been passed asking for 'a motor omnibus service in Sea Road (Boscombe)'. The Borough Surveyor was promptly instructed 'to report upon the expediency of supplying such a service between Lansdowne and The Pier, and The Square and The Pier Approach'. Alarmed by the implications of a Bill in Parliamentary Committee in May of that year, the Council asked the MP for Bournemouth to support the principle that railway companies should not be given the unrestricted power to run omnibuses which had been refused

◄ The tale of Bournemouth Tramways' first motorbus carries a hint of intrigue. Straker & MacConnell (no connection with Straker-Squire), formed only that year, won the contract in December 1905, against 11 competitors, to supply 'two cars at £980 each'. One arrived, and the Council clearly thought it was a Berna. But this wooden-wheeled hybrid was most likely assembled from bits of Arbenz, Bianchi, Lacoste & Battmann, or Rapid of Turin — with a Berna radiator. The bodywork, however, was by Knight of Dorchester, and this bore the registration number EL 366. *David L. Chalk collection*

The hybrid chassis was delivered with an additional closed 28-seat omnibus body; and it is this combination whose details are recorded in the Heavy Vehicle Register on 28 March 1906 and which entered service between Boscombe Arcade and Boscombe Pier that spring (the extra-long axle-stub identifying this as EL 366 appears at rear, top right). Parked at the entrance of Sea Road, some of its details are obscured by the conductor and a diminutive figure in a long dress, but enough is visible to identify a rear platform and 4½-bay bodywork. *Colin Morris collection*

municipal corporations, and that there should be some local control and supervision. Clearly, the councillors foresaw the London & South Western Railway's extending beyond its rails to compete with the trams in Bournemouth.

In November 1905 the surveyor was instructed by the Council to obtain specifications and estimates for two cars for 'a proposed motor car service to Boscombe Pier'. The Rev Ebben's request had been approved, and something larger than wagonette was being sought. Twelve companies tendered: manufacturers Glover Bros Ltd of London; Simms of Kilburn, De Dion Bouton Ltd, Clarkson Ltd of Chelmsford; Sidney Straker & Squire Ltd of Bristol, The Lancashire Steam Motor Co (Leyland), Milnes Daimler of Wellington, Salop, and Durham Churchill & Co of Attercliffe, Sheffield, and supply agents Neave & Hussey of St Peter's Road, Bournemouth, The Motor Car Emporium, London, and 'Andrew Brothers'. There was also a bid from a small company with more ambition than substance, called Straker & MacConnell of Avonmore Road, West Kensington. Straker & MacConnell had been registered as a private company in March of that year with seven subscribers, notably Hugh MacConnell, his wife Jessie and son James. Among the rest was Leonard Herbert Straker, described as an engineer, whose name took precedence in the firm's title. This considerably irked Sidney Straker of Straker & Squire Ltd (a competitor for the Bournemouth order), which company alleged misrepresentation and pursued the matter in an entertaining court case. On 31 March 1906

Straker & MacConnell was unable to 'complete' the second bus. The London manager of Berna came to inspect the existing chassis in November 1906, and it seems highly likely that he supplied a complete new Berna chassis and took the original bits and pieces away. Certainly, in this photograph taken at the eastern end of Southcote Road depot in 1907, this is a proper Swiss-built Berna chassis — with cast metal wheels and high-set bonnet-line. It carries the same open body and registration. *Colin Morris collection*

the smaller firm was re-registered as Straker & MacConnell (1906) Ltd, its board comprising Hugh and James MacConnell and three completely new directors. Leonard Straker had gone — his contribution apparently complete. The firm declared itself sole agent for Berna of Olten and Arbenz of Zurich, for Bianchi & Co of Milan, the Societa Torinese Automobile Rapid (STAR) of Turin and for Lacoste & Battmann of Paris. It imported components from these firms and assembled at least one taxicab and a motor lorry which it exhibited under its own name — before being wound up in July 1907.

Straker & MacConnell, then, was the firm which won the Bournemouth contract to supply 'two Cars at £980 each . . . subject to their bodies being similar in all respects to that inspected at the De Dion stand by the Surveyor and Chairman of the Tramways Committee at the recent . . . Olympia [show]'. What they had seen was a De Dion (EL 316) fitted with a canopied charabanc body by A. Knight & Co of Dorchester, smartly turned out in (prophetically) yellow and blue for Eugene Poulain of the Haven Hotel, Sandbanks (and thus giving rise to the notion that Bournemouth's first bus was a De Dion).
By January 1906 the surveyor had obtained an amended estimate providing a saving of £70 per car, enabling the Council to buy an additional covered bus body. The Committee was 'driven over the district' in this version of the bus mounted upon the one chassis which Straker & MacConnell was able to complete and deliver. It was registered EL 366 — the number also applied to the charabanc body. An iron building, 20ft by 24ft, was erected at Southcote Road depot to house the chassis and bodies. Straker & MacConnell failed to assemble a second chassis, however, and the Council cancelled its order in April 1906. It seems that the Traffic Manager may have hired a motorbus by the day when EL 366 was undergoing its numerous repairs, and this may explain the unidentified registration number EL 480 in Corporation records.

In November 1906 Berna's London manager inspected the one chassis operating and informed Barber, the Traffic Manager, that he was 'quite prepared to put in necessary new parts free of charge'. Judging by photographic evidence, however, he replaced the wooden-wheeled hybrid completely with a proper metal-wheeled Swiss-built Berna, which also bore the registration number EL 366 and continued the operation of the Corporation's only bus service at that time, the length of Sea Road between Boscombe Arcade and Boscombe Pier.

The Berna continued its lonely existence on this summer-only service until, in February 1910, it was discovered that it would cost some £250-300 to put into working order and that, in any case, it would not be ready for Easter. The new General Manager, Charles Hill, met the Managing Director of Leyland, who agreed to let out on hire a chassis fitted with petrol-electric drive, for £10 per week — that to include all running costs and the wages of a man sent to drive and take charge of the bus, which would be fitted with the Council's charabanc body. It could be hired for as long as was necessary for testing purposes, when it would be available for purchase.

All negotiations for hire were then undertaken via the Thomas Transmission Co Ltd of Croydon, which extended the hiring until the end of August 1910. In June, however, it removed its 'Leyland Thomas' chassis for demonstration to another potential customer, although it seems to have been returned in time for the Corporation's centenary celebrations (version 1). The loan was

▲ Even the Berna began to feel the strain of climbing Sea Road from Boscombe Pier and, in April 1910, the bodywork was again retained whilst the chassis was replaced by a considerably different machine. The Council hired a Leyland fitted with petrol-electric drive made by the Thomas Transmission Co Ltd, which sent down its 'own man' to drive it as part of the deal. He sits at the wheel as the vehicle waits at Boscombe Pier and the Corporation driver is left patting the radiator.
Colin Morris collection

Despite the 9 May 1910 entry in the Heavy Vehicle Register — 'EL 366 "Leyland Thomas" patent drive 40hp electric-petrol open type' — there is no pictorial evidence that this combination carried that number. As may be seen in this three-quarter rear view, the chassis brought its proper registration (LN 9894) to Bournemouth and wore it too. Thomas's 'man', whose wages were included in the £10-per-week hire of the vehicle, has now decided to permit the Corporation crew to sit in front. *Alan Lambert collection*

not extended beyond September, however, and the experimental chassis was returned to Croydon. Bournemouth Corporation's first flirtation with the motorbus was over.

Bournemouth had no further motorbus in its service until 1914, by which time the appropriate technology had come on by leaps and bounds. The focus of attention had moved westward in September 1913 when a motorbus from Westbourne to the sea end of Alumhurst Road was considered, and, in February 1914, tenders from Tilling-Stevens, Scout, Straker-Squire, Wolseley, Leyland, Daimler and the Imperial Motor Works (agents in Bournemouth) were considered. The Committee examined a double-deck Tilling Stevens and a single-deck Daimler. Trials were held on Sea Road on 5 February. The following day, a Scout single-decker and a Leyland double-decker were examined. The members then met in the generating station's reading room and decided to order two Tilling-Stevens double-deckers (EL 2103/4) and two Daimler saloon buses (EL 2105/6) — £910 and £908 each respectively — all with Brush bodywork. One Tilling-Stevens ran on the original Sea Road, Boscombe, route from 30 April 1914; the other was tried on a Charminster Road service but ran at a heavy loss. The Daimlers worked upon the planned Alum Chine route from 25 May and on an experimental route from The Square to Bournemouth Pier from 8 July. Several variations were tried, but an overall deficit was run up which had to be borne by the Tramways profit margin. Worse was to come. The onset of World War 1 nipped further expansion in the bud as 25% of the Tramways staff joined the colours but were kept on half pay. From October 1914 only the Westbourne Arcade–Alum Chine bus was in service.

In November 1914 the War Office commandeered the two Daimler chassis. The saloon bodies and registration numbers were transferred to two new Tilling-Stevens petrol-electric chassis bought with the £1,404 compensation payment received in January 1915, and these entered service in April. By the autumn,

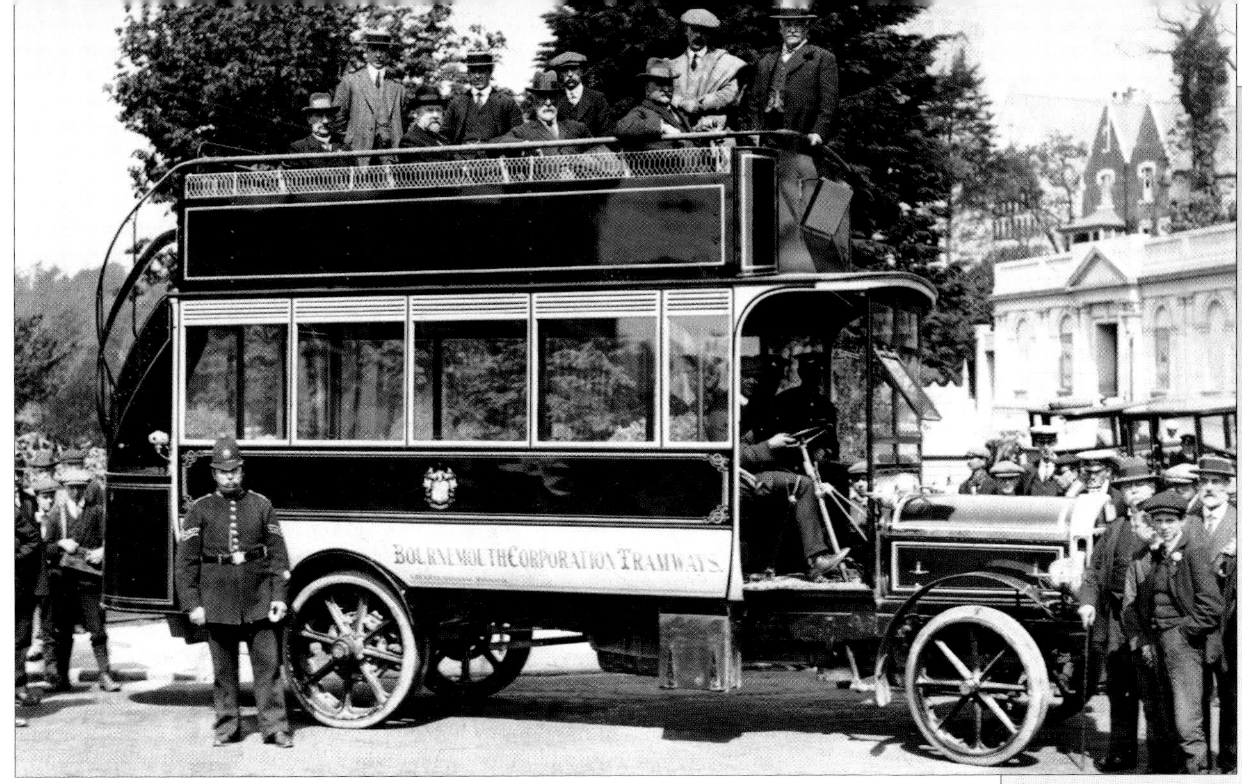

◂ Having failed to sell its chassis to Bournemouth, Thomas took it away before the end of the 1910 summer season, and the Council began to think about 'trackless trolleys' instead. The town went without a motorbus until 1914, when it tested a Tilling-Stevens and a Daimler on the Sea Road route and decided to purchase two of each, the bodywork to be by Brush. This is Tilling-Stevens EL 2103, costing £910, prior to operating on the Sea Road route.
David L. Chalk collection

◂ Photographed in Leicestershire prior to delivery from the Brush works is Daimler EL 2105, fitted with a 4¼-bay saloon body, similar in pattern to the one worn by the chassis delivered by Straker & MacConnell, save for its flush sides and forward-facing seats. These two Daimlers had an extremely short life in Bournemouth — from May until November 1914, when the War Office took both chassis for military service, but paid considerably more than they had cost new.
David L. Chalk collection

▲ What looks like a double-decker bus is not: the Brush saloon bodywork and registration number EL 2106 has been transferred (in January 1915) to a make which the military did not seek to requisition — Tilling-Stevens. The panelling fitted above window level was a temporary affair designed to stop a partly-inflated gas bag flopping off the roof. The bus was running on coal gas, in an effort to save petrol for the Army's war effort. *David L. Chalk collection*

200 staff had joined the military and the employment of women conductors was approved. During the winter months which followed a lorry body was fixed to chassis EL 2105, which was used successfully for carting purposes. Despite his clear preference for trams, Bulfin retained the four Tilling-Stevens, although two of them (EL 2103/5) became tower wagons for the overhead linesmen. EL 2106 was converted to burn coal gas and staggered on in its stage-carriage rôle.

Thus the quartet survived the war, to be joined in 1920 by four further Tilling-Stevens TS3 Brush-bodied saloons. These too ran at a loss — which must have come as something of a disappointment for that motorbus pioneer Councillor Francis J. Bell, who retired that year after nearly a decade as Chairman of the Tramways Committee.

The financial breakthrough for motorbuses came following a 1923 decision to purchase 'runabouts' for a service along the new Undercliff Drive between Bournemouth and Boscombe piers; the Council had nearly opted to place them in the care of the Beach Committee, but the latter decided to settle for a rental arrangement whereby it would receive a regular payment for the use of its Undercliff Drive. The local coachbuilder J. & A. Steane won the contract to supply the six vehicles at just over £600 each. These were 16-seater 'toastracks' with Guy chassis and solid tyres. The first three started work on 23 July 1923 at a flat fare of 6d and stayed in 'summer service' until 6 December. Their gross surplus of £1,531 was considered so successful that, when the second trio entered service in 1924, the fare was reduced to 4d with 2d intermediate stages — and the profit margin increased as a result. Even Bulfin was impressed.

It had become apparent that small-capacity, low-cost vehicles used in an attractive location could produce good results. The Committee could hardly have failed to notice that, since July 1924, Dean & Barrett of Swanage had been running a very popular service on the Purbeck peninsula with what it called a 'Moto-tram' — a Shelvoke & Drewry 'Freighter', as that manufacturer titled its product, designed

More modern Tilling-Stevens joined the fleet in 1920, but all motorbuses ran at a deficit until 1923, when the first of six Guy J 'Runabouts' was delivered. These were placed on service between Bournemouth and Boscombe piers, running along the Undercliff Drive — for which the Tramways Committee was obliged to pay the Beach Committee £300 per annum. EL 8129 and its five companions had run up a profit of £1,646 by 1925 — despite the rent! *David S. Deacon*

Convinced that small was beautiful, so far as motorbuses were concerned, the Council decided — in May 1925 — to try its luck with Shelvoke & Drewry Tramocars. In September 1925, two joined the Undercliff Drive service, but extended it at both ends, to Bournemouth Pier and to Boscombe Arcade. RU 2267 was one of six Tramocars with Chalmers 20-seat bodywork in service by 1926. Again, a profit-maker had been found, to reduce the overall motorbus deficit. *David S. Deacon*

A Strachan & Brown-bodied W. & G. du Cros 26-seat saloon pauses beside the 'Duke of Argyll's scratching posts' in The Square, whilst an earlier du Cros-bodied example comes around to join it. A total of 15 saloons of this make were purchased, some of them to cope with increased demand created by the opening of the new Pavilion in Westover. Each cost in the region of £1,157, but they were outlasted in service by the Tramocars. *David S. Deacon*

primarily as a small dustcart chassis. On 7 May 1925, however, the Committee inspected a Hickman-bodied example, which was tested on Bath Hill. From that date onward they referred to the type as a 'Tramocar', which means that the demonstrator was almost certainly PX 886 of Walter Gates' 'Waterfront' service at Worthing. 'Tramocar' was his chosen fleetname, carried fore and aft, and Bournemouth simply adopted it for the six which they were now to purchase. These were Chalmers-bodied 20-seaters, double-doored, and costing £855 each. The first two started a through service from The Square to Boscombe Arcade via the Undercliff Drive on 18 September 1925. They too operated at a profit, together with the four which followed.

During the winter months the Tramocars sometimes replaced larger buses at Westbourne and Boscombe, trailing the sound of their tram-type gongs behind them. During the period 1929-31 they and the Guys were fitted with pneumatic tyres, and these two types went on making profits until withdrawal in 1938 and 1937 respectively. Only one Tramocar blotted its copybook: on 20 July 1932 No 9 (RU 2266) ran away on Boscombe Pier Approach and fell onto the beach, killing two people and leaving several others injured. Brake failure was blamed. Meanwhile, in 1925, three new Tilling-Stevens TS6 37-seaters, costing £1,700 each, arrived to cover parts of tram routes during a major track-relaying programme.

In 1927 the Council bought three W. & G. du Cros 26-seat saloons with bodywork by the chassis builder. A further nine with similar bodies by Strachan & Brown were added in 1928, followed by three with Hall Lewis coachwork at £1,157 each, the latter to meet expected demand in connection with the opening of the new Pavilion in 1929. On 19 June of that year, the Committee inspected and took trial runs in four six-wheeled single-deck demonstrators — a Guy, a Halley, a Karrier and a Thornycroft, each with 40 seats. The choice fell upon the Karrier WL6/1 model, and five with dual-door bodywork by Hall Lewis, at £1,785 apiece, were duly delivered. At about this time a service to Alma Road was extended to Victoria Avenue and Boundary Road, the Cranleigh Road route being extended to Tuckton Bridge.

The idea of an express bus service in connection with trams was inaugurated in Manchester in 1927. This was in response to complaints from tram passengers in outlying districts that a very large amount of their time was wasted at intermediate tram stops. In December 1929 Bournemouth planned a similar provision. Since Bournemouth had no powers to run buses outside its own boundaries, such a service could not go into Christchurch or Poole. The express buses were to stop at fare stages only; otherwise they would be competing with the trams.

The competition to provide the necessary vehicles attracted much interest, and on 17 January at Southcote Road depot, Committee members inspected 10 vehicles; AEC, Crossley, Guy, Halley, Karrier, Leyland, Sunbeam Motor Car Co Ltd, Thornycroft, Vulcan and W. & G. du Cros were represented. This time, Thornycroft was successful, and an initial 12 BCF types with dual-door bodywork, by Strachans (Acton) Ltd (4),

A brave decision was made in March 1929 — to purchase five (then) large-capacity six-wheeled buses. They were to be equipped with dual doors for ease of loading and off-loading when the trippers were in town — an idea borrowed from the Tramocars and which became a Bournemouth standard for many decades afterwards. Winner of the contract was Karrier, with its WL6/1 chassis, fitted with Hall Lewis bodywork, costing £1,785 each. *Philip Davies collection*

Beadle (4) and local firm J. Martin (4), each with 32 seats and costing some £1,400 per vehicle, were delivered by Easter 1930.

Three express routes were launched on 17 April 1930: County Gates–Tuckton, which was curtailed at the West Station on 16 June and once again to The Square on 31 July, as the main weight of passenger demand became apparent (extended to Christchurch on 6 November 1930); The Square–Moordown (extended to Kinson on 15 December 1930 and on to Bear Cross on 1 August 1931), extended to Bournemouth Pier on 1 November 1932; and The Lansdowne–King's Road, which was withdrawn completely on 15 June 1930, the demand having been over-estimated. Those extensions in brackets above were given Ministry of Transport consent under Section 104 of the Bournemouth Corporation Act 1930. Because the Borough boundary was to be pushed westward to encompass Wallisdown, East and West Howe, Cudnell, Kinson and Ensbury — all previously in Dorset — Hants & Dorset was obliged to transfer to the Corporation its service from Winton to Wallisdown. Additionally, the Corporation was empowered to operate buses beyond Tuckton Bridge to Church Street, Christchurch, and over Iford Bridge to Church Street, Castle Street and on to Purewell, for which Hants & Dorset was to be compensated. However, Corporation inspectors were empowered to board Hants & Dorset buses to check a special range of tickets, overprinted 'BCT', which were to be supplied to the company by the Corporation. With minor modifications, these were to remain in use until 31 December 1970, during which time Hants & Dorset was to charge any passenger both taken up and set down within this expanded 'Corporation Area' the same fare he would have been charged on a Corporation bus — but to retain only the operating costs. The rest would be paid to the Corporation in accumulated amounts every six months.

To run these new services Bournemouth purchased a further 12 Thornycroft BCF/Beadle 32-seaters, for which a reduced price of £1,370 each was charged. Having taken over what had

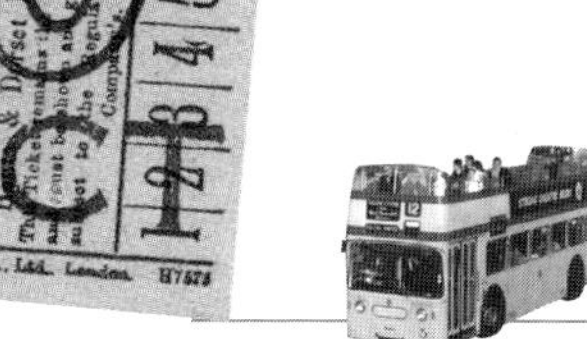

In December 1929 the Council decided that it would introduce a series of express motorbus routes within its territory designed to speed up journey times for longer-distance passengers. In January 1930, Thornycroft was awarded a contract which resulted in the delivery of 24 BCF-type saloons, seating 32 apiece, to Bournemouth Corporation. LJ 3003 was a Beadle-bodied example: others had coachwork by Strachans or J. Martin of Bournemouth.
Colin Morris collection

▲ been Hants & Dorset's route 9, the Corporation decided to number all its omnibus routes (the trams did not carry route numbers), the number to be shown front and side initially and illuminated at night, and in 1931 to give fleet numbers to its bus fleet, which, since 1927, had been entirely single-deck. To mark the increased proportion of motorbuses in its rolling stock, in April 1931 the title 'Bournemouth Corporation Tramways & Motor Services' was altered to 'Bournemouth Corporation Transport Services', and the Tramways Committee was re-named the Transport Committee.

The first covered-top double-decker buses were six AECs with 48-seat English Electric bodies featuring dual entrance/exits and staircases — an arrangement which became standard in the fleet until the early 'Sixties. They came to Bournemouth in 1932 with advertisements on the windows singing the praises of the town as a health resort; they were received in style at the Town Hall, and three of them, dressed with flags, participated in the ceremonial opening of the new Iford Bridge on 10 February 1933. There was then a six-year period when all double-deck additions were trolley-buses, ending with the acquisition of three second-hand AEC Regents with Park Royal bodywork — ex-Southampton Nos 2, 3 and 5. In 1940 they were rebodied with 29-seat Beadle saloon bodies removed from Thornycroft chassis, and were rebodied yet again with Northern Counties 56-seat utility bodies in 1944.

In 1937/8 nine Bedford WTBs with 25-seat Duple bodywork started working the less heavily-trafficked routes, and were joined in 1938/9 by 16 further WTBs with special coachwork by Burlingham designed for the more scenic coastal routes. The last of the inter-war years also saw the arrival of a chassis/coachwork combination which many consider the most attractively designed double-decker to have served the Corporation; Nos 17-32 were Leyland Titan TD5 types with 48-seat, full-fronted Weymann bodies featuring the usual twin staircases. In recognition of their dedication to sunny Bournemouth, they were also fitted with an opening sunshine roof, a very popular feature. Like Eastbourne, Bournemouth had decided that the comparatively quiet-running petrol engine was more appropriate to its gracious image, so these beautiful Titans were not re-fitted with diesel engines until the middle 'Fifties. Eventually, six of them would be converted into open-toppers, finally retiring in 1965, after more than a quarter-century of service.

Over 30 of the Corporation's motorbuses were commandeered for military and other emergency purposes in World War 2, including all seven of the 1937 Bedford saloons. With so many trolleybuses sent to serve elsewhere, Bournemouth was left somewhat short when members of the military — notably Canadian servicemen — began to be billeted in the town. This difficulty was eased in the winter of 1942/3 with the arrival of what became that wartime classic, the Bedford OWB utility saloon. Three were bodied by Duple and three to the same angular design by Mulliner. They were joined in their efforts during 1943 by six open-staircase AEC Tilling ST-type double-deckers hired from London Transport in their red and cream livery.

Bournemouth was also allotted four Guy Arab I 6LW double-deck utilities bodied by Park Royal and four Arab II 5LW models by Weymann, each in grey with maroon bands, and featuring the no-frills, lobster-backed construction. The Corporation had four of its AEC Regents rebodied in the same style by Northern Coachbuilders in 1944/5. All buses had had 'BOURNEMOUTH CORPORATION' removed from their waistbands earlier in the war (in case German parachutists landed and discovered where they were) and, like the trolleybuses, received a matt bauxite roof coating if they were not in the wartime grey livery. The war period ended in 1945 with the acquisition of six ex-Huddersfield Corporation AEC Regent double-deckers. Three entered service in a grey livery as buses, one was used solely as spares and two were converted for use as tower wagons to maintain the trolleybus overhead.

Postwar, Bournemouth Corporation was beset, as were all other operators, by a shortage of materials and staff, and, as the obstacles

◄ Having seen Hants & Dorset's covered-top buses steal an expensive march over its open-topped trams in the Borough of Poole, Bournemouth for some time toyed with the idea of buying some of its own. At last, in January 1932, it decided to buy six AEC Regent 48-seater double-deckers with English Electric bodywork — its first dual-door double-deckers. With necessary spares, they cost £1,536 each. This view is within the Southcote Road depot. *David L. Chalk collection*

◄ Conscious of the need to buy something a little 'sporty' to show off the delights of Bournemouth to its increasing number of visitors, the Corporation bought nine Bedford WTB/Duple saloons in 1937/8. It added 16 more, to an uprated specification and bodied by Burlingham, in 1938/9. Pictured when new, and showing off its sightseeing quarterlights, is No 13 (FEL 216), one of the Burlingham-bodied batch — incidentally, the vehicle upon which David Chalk learned to drive a bus. *David L. Chalk collection*

Swinging around past the Royal Bath Hotel and into Westover Road comes Leyland Titan TD5 No 19 (FEL 202), one of 16 much-admired high-specification double-deckers by Weymann. They were fitted with 'sunshine' sliding roofs, beautifully-appointed interiors and other refinements. World War 2 dampened their potential somewhat but probably helped some of them to remain in service for over 25 years.
Mac Cooper collection

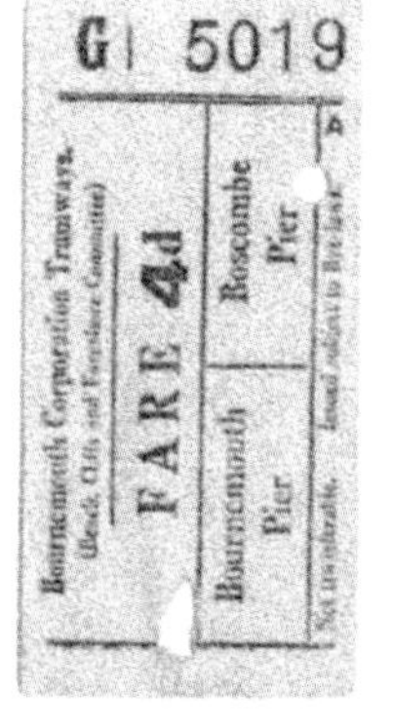

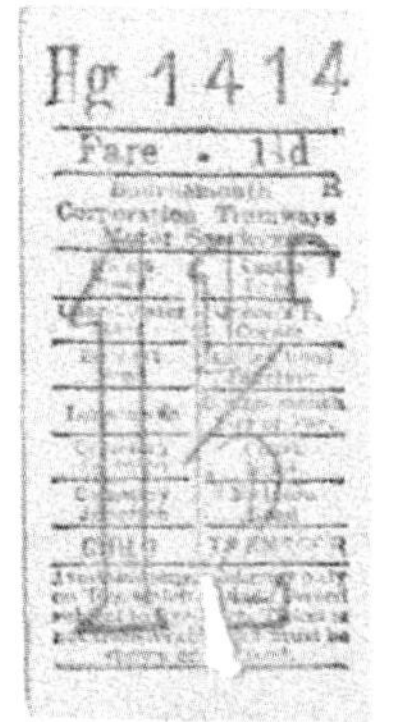

Bb 1674

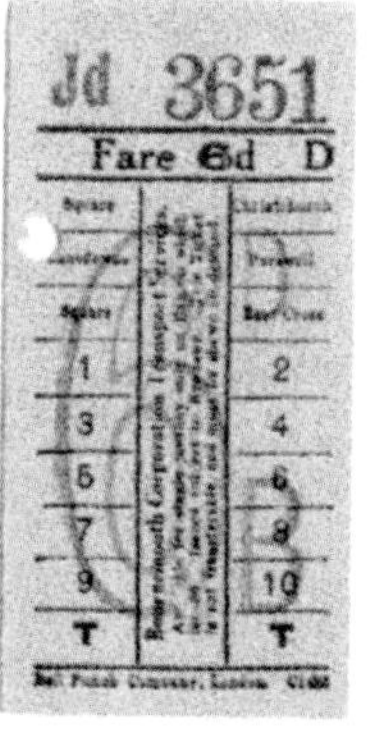

were removed from the beach and tourists began to flood back to the resort, the Transport Department was at full stretch. Planning continued, however, and as new housing estates grew so they were added to the network of bus services, and in June 1949 the coastal route between Bournemouth Pier and Hengistbury Head was restored.

The first sign that things were really getting back to normal was the Council's decision to invest in three luxury coaches to be employed principally upon a new summer service. These were Leyland PS2/1 Tigers with full-fronted 32-seat coachwork by Burlingham — so attractive that all three have survived in preservation (two in the care of the Bournemouth Passenger Transport Association). Purchased in 1949, they launched the circular tour of Bournemouth from the Pier Approach on 3 July 1950 and served the Corporation for 20 years.

Leyland's impressive new diesel engine — a derivative of its tank power unit developed in World War 2 — was also employed in the Titan PD2/3 double-decker. The arrival of 30 of these — Bournemouth's first 8ft-wide buses — in 1950 kick-started the expansion of services reaching

Again a producer of many military vehicles, Guy was one of the few companies chosen to build double-decker bus chassis during the war. The angular, no-frills bodywork is evident in this picture of No 35 (FRU 182), a 6LW-powered Guy Arab I, photographed in Bourne Avenue during the late 'Fifties. Bodywork was by Park Royal for the four Arab I models and by Weymann for the five-cylinder Mk II quartet which followed. When delivered they had wooden slatted seats and a grey livery with maroon bands. *Mac Cooper collection*

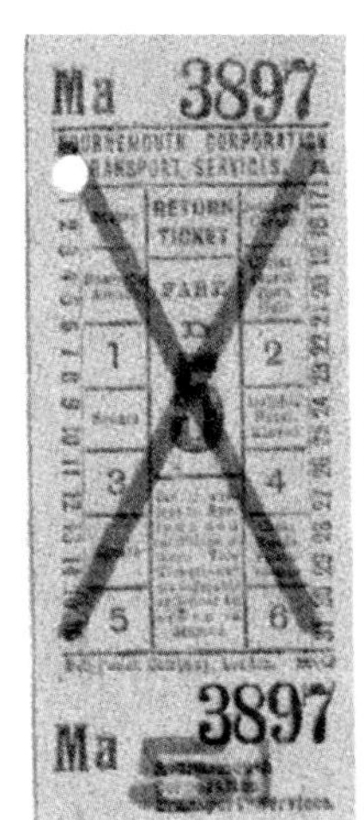

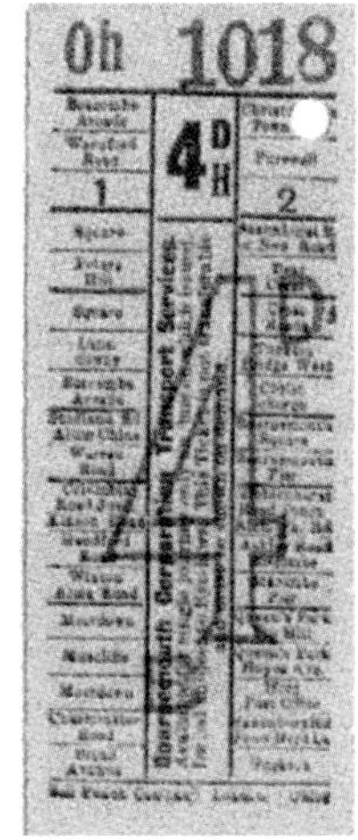

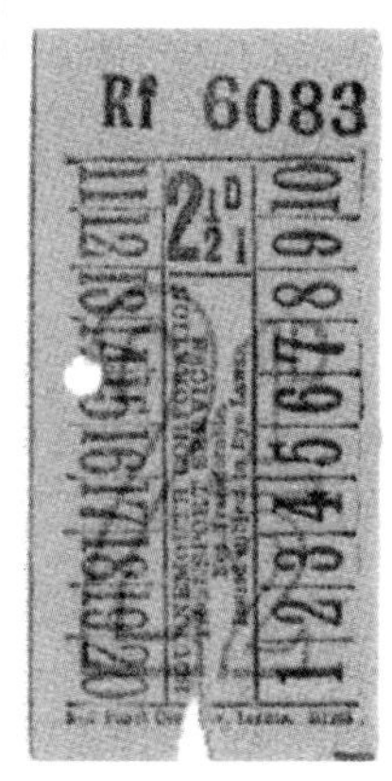

The first motorbuses to run at a profit for Bournemouth Corporation were the Guy runabouts on service between Bournemouth and Boscombe piers. The 4d ticket, bearing the title of the Beach, Cliffs & Foreshore Committee in addition to 'Bournemouth Corporation Tramways', was issued in May 1924. The fare for the journey along the Undercliff Drive had been reduced that month from 6d as a result of its commercial success. Andrew Waller writes: 'Bournemouth's bus tickets were in a different range of colours from the trams — and the trolleybuses until the 1940s. The numbered stage tickets that replaced the "geographical" ones were [then] used on both buses and trolleybuses. There was a special range of early morning returns — to be issued before 8.45am — allowing the return journey to be made on either a Corporation bus or a Hants & Dorset.' *Andrew H. Waller collection*

Vehicle supplies dried up during the war as manufacturers went over to the production of military vehicles. Bedford was one of those firms, producing thousands of trucks and engines, but was chosen to construct the standard single-decker 32-seat bus — the OWB model. In the winter of 1942/3 Bournemouth received six: No 187 (FRU 105) had bodywork by Mulliner to the approved utility pattern. In May 1953 it was converted into this open style for 'sight-seeing' work. It retained its wooden seats. *G. O. Pearce/Ian Allan Library*

At the end of the war, three second-hand AEC Regent double-deckers joined the passenger fleet, and it was not until 1949 that something more luxurious was purchased. The choice was quite radical: three luxuriously-appointed coaches with coachwork by the Blackpool bodybuilder Burlingham. The chassis were of the Leyland Tiger PS2/1 type with diesel engines. No 45 (JLJ 402) is at the Pier, collecting passengers for the Special Circular Tour which was established by these vehicles. *Colin Morris collection*

beyond the trolleybus system. The vehicles were impressive too, but the Weymann bodywork was, perhaps, less pretty than that of the prewar Titans. The PD2/3s nevertheless matched the service record of the Tigers, and four of them are in preservation (three with the BPTA and one with Mac Cooper). Burlingham of Blackpool was again the preferred coachbuilder for the first underfloor-engined vehicles in the fleet, delivered in the winter of 1953/4. These were six Leyland Royal Tiger PSU1/13 41-seat saloons, primarily for use on the more scenic routes. Of equal carrying capacity, but of lighter construction, and this time bodied by Park Royal, were six 1955 Leyland Tiger Cub PSUC1/1 saloons. These were also underfloor-engined and were bought to participate in the tourist traffic during the summer, as well as performing more prosaic duties at other times.

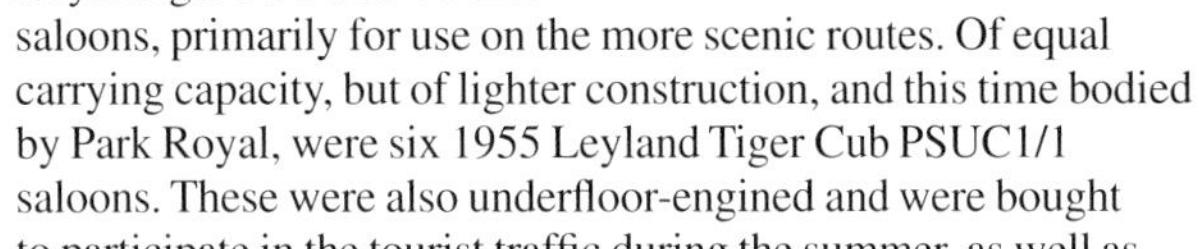

The new vehicles were purchased on a wave of confidence following the carriage of the largest number of passengers in the undertaking's history in 1950. The figures then diminished gradually until, from 1955 onward, private means of transport began to increase by leaps and bounds, fewer people went to the cinema as television began to take hold, and the five-day (rather than six) working week was introduced. Adjustments to schedules, the variation of routes to serve new housing estates, extensions here, contractions there, plus cost-saving exercises, may be traced back to this period.

There was a four-year gap in new motorbus deliveries until 1959 when the first of 20 Leyland PD3/1 Titans arrived to replace older vehicles being retired. These were the last built for Bournemouth with the twin-staircase arrangement. A programme for the removal of the front staircases of earlier Titans was subsequently put in train, and this policy was also extended to 10 trolleybuses. The 1963 delivery of 10 Leyland Titan PD3A/1/Weymann 68-seaters represented the monetary advantage of such a policy.

As elsewhere, rear-engined double-decker buses were chosen to replace the trolleybuses, but delays in production encountered at the outset meant that Leyland Titans had to take part the initial programme. Indeed, a rather frustrated Department was obliged to obtain its first two Daimler Fleetlines (40/1) from an unusual source. These had bodywork built in Northern Ireland and were diverted from Belfast Corporation in 1964. Ten Leyland Atlanteans followed that November and 20 Daimler Fleetlines — 10 of which were convertible open-toppers — arrived in 1965. Those with detachable tops (180-9) came as a bit of an afterthought following a slight embarrassment. A prewar Titan converted to open-top had refused to go up Priory Hill with its load of passengers and its conductor had to ask them to walk and be picked up again at the top; the type was promptly retired. Ian Cunningham: 'For this batch of Fleetlines I devised two or three lists of names of local worthies I thought had contributed to the history of Bournemouth, and presented them to the Transport Committee, but for some unknown reason or other they were not acceptable and we finished up with "county" names instead.' Three Weymann-bodied Leopards also arrived in 1965, these were fitted with 45 coach seats, cove windows and extra coach-style trim to make them suitable for use on town tours.

A further 20 Atlanteans (200-19), this time with MCW bodywork, rather than the Weymann specified for the earlier deliveries due to closure of the latter, arrived in 1966. There then came a remarkable period of standardisation, lasting from 1969 to 1981, during which all 126 Leyland or Daimler double-deckers delivered were fitted with gradually-evolving 74-seat bodywork by Walter Alexander & Co (Coachbuilders) Ltd of Falkirk — an association described by that manufacturer as 'much valued'.

The first tentative steps toward rebuilding a fleet of single-deck buses were taken in 1967/8 with the purchase of 11 Daimler

PAVILION
LOUNGE BAR
PALACE COURT HOTEL
CIRCULAR TOUR
15
JLJ402

▼ Bournemouth Corporation Transport got into full stride again with the order for 30 Leyland PD2/3 double-deckers with 48-seat Weymann bodywork. At last the operator was able to carry on, in a big way, the full-fronted theme that started with the Titans delivered in 1939 but was brought to a halt by war. No 114 (KEL 114) is pictured in Gervis Place with BUT trolleybus No 215. As delivered, the PD2/3 Titans had Bournemouth's standard double-staircase layout.
Mac Cooper collection

▲ In 1959 a batch of 10 Leyland Titan PD3/1 double-deckers with what was known in the trade as 'BMMO fronts' (the radiator grilles) and with Weymann 62-seat bodywork was delivered. These were followed by another 10 in 1960. No 162 (6162 RU), however, was a Titan PD3A/1, one of 10 further Weymann-bodied Leylands with 'St Helens' fronts, delivered in 1963. Because these were front-entrance only, each offered room for six more passengers.
Southdown Enthusiasts' Club

◄ Parked in the entrance to Gervis Place is the last of six Leyland PSU1/13 41-seaters delivered in 1953. Originally numbered 262, No 94 (NLJ 272) had dual doorways when delivered, with an open platform at the rear. In 1960 this was 'filled in' as part of a conversion programme for one-man operation. The Burlingham bodywork featured 'observation' coving windows for use on sightseeing routes during the summer months and, from 1964, was fitted with a public-address system.
Mac Cooper collection

Epitomising Bournemouth as a seaside resort is this photograph of open-top Daimler Fleetline CRG6/Weymann No 182 (CRU 182C) seen at Boscombe Pier. This was one of a batch of 10 convertible open-toppers delivered in 1965 and was originally named *Warwickshire*. In October 1977 seven of these passed to London Transport for use on the Round London Sightseeing tour, No 182 becoming DMO1 in the LTE fleet. *Mac Cooper*

In October 1980, No 241 (SEL 241H), a 1970 Atlantean with Alexander bodywork, passes the Royal Bath Hotel, which could claim to have been Bournemouth's first (horse) bus depot. The vehicle is wearing the short-lived 'blue flash' logos — a livery beatifully reflected in the hotel commissionaire's uniform as he watches its progress towards The Square. *Colin Morris*

In 1955 six additional 41-seat saloons, with dual doors and observation windows at roof level, joined what, in effect, was the dual-purpose single-deck part of the Bournemouth fleet. These were Leyland Tiger Cub PSUC1/1 models with Park Royal coachwork. Pictured on its first day of service — 1 October 1955 — is No 264 (RRU 901) operating on route No 4 between Kings Road and Lansdowne. The batch, Nos 263-8, would be renumbered 95-100 between May 1958 and April 1959, having already been rebuilt to single-door layout for one-man operation in 1957/8. *G. O. P. Pearce*

Originally No 39, one of the wartime Guy Arab II 5LW utility double-deckers, No 16 (FRU 223) underwent two drastic alterations in appearance during its lengthy stay in Bournemouth. First, in 1953, it had its roof and upper-deck windows removed to become an open-top double decker. Then, in June 1959, it had a further transformation into a 35-seat open single-decker. No 38 joined it in this guise five years later, and the pair became known locally as 'The Banana Boats'. *David L. Chalk collection*

◂ The influx of rear-engined double-deckers began unexpectedly with two buses diverted from Belfast Corporation and with bodies by MH Coachworks of Northern Ireland. No 41 (ALJ 341B), a Daimler Fleetline CRG6, was one of them, delivered in 1964. No 190 (CRU 190C) is a 1965 CRG6 with Weymann bodywork and No 211 (HEL 211D) a Leyland Atlantean PDR1/1 Mk II with Metro-Cammell body of 1966. A 1972 Alexander-bodied Atlantean coasts down Avenue Road, as a Vespa scooter buzzes through The Triangle. *Colin Morris*

Roadliner/Willowbrook 49-seaters. By 1976, four coaches and six minibuses were in service. A further three minibuses, including a battery-powered Dodge were delivered in 1979. On the double-deck front, Marshall of Cambridge was the coachbuilder which broke the mould in 1981/2 when it was chosen to provide 78-seat bodywork for 20 Leyland Olympians.

Borough councils nationally lost their 'Corporation' status in 1973. Bournemouth chose to amend its fleet title to 'Bournemouth Transport' and to abandon the maroon bands around its vehicles. Instead, it adopted an azure-blue circle as a background for this new identity, which encompassed the Borough coat of arms. A blue flash sprang from each side of the circle. This device was, however, short-lived. As Ian Cunningham recalls, 'Around about 1980 we asked our marketing agents what the public thought about Bournemouth Transport, as we called it at that time . . . they carried out interviews on the street and with in-house groups, quite extensively, and they found that people in Bournemouth were generally well-disposed toward their transport undertaking. They thought that the staff did their job well and that the buses were clean and comfortable. But it was they who said "Why don't you call them 'Yellow Buses'?" All the public call them "Yellow Buses" — and so [from 1982] we did!'

A growing coach fleet at the same time became 'Yellow Coaches', both fleetnames being displayed in brown, and blue made what proved to be a temporary disappearance from Bournemouth Transport vehicles. Ken Baily, a famous Bournemouth character, spearheaded the attendant publicity campaign in its first year, to be replaced in 1983 by the Bournemouth Symphony Orchestra. A leaflet which befitted Bournemouth's 'health' image — 'Get around on the Yellows' — was published, inviting people to visit a selection of public houses by bus, rather than drinking and driving themselves. A dip in passenger levels was largely arrested, and sales of off-peak Money Saver and season tickets increased.

The last new vehicles to enter service under the Council's direct control were five Volvos with double-deck coach bodywork by East Lancs. They were delivered between July and September 1986, just weeks before a radical change came into effect countrywide.

Delivered in 1971, No 263 (ULJ 263J) was one of a batch of 16 Leyland Atlantean PDR1A/1s. Bodywork was by Alexander and originally carried the two maroon bands lined with Brunswick green. However, when this atmospheric photograph was taken on 26 September 1985, it was dressed in the early style of Yellow Buses livery. The bus is climbing the lower part of Old Christchurch Road *en route* to Fisherman's Walk and Tuckton Bridge. *D. E. Wall*

In 1973 Ian Cunningham, General Manager and advocate of electric traction, got a free three-month loan of a Morrison battery-electric bus. Because of its weight, principally, it was not the success hoped for, but it established the idea of the 'Town Centre Service' — a figure-of-eight route around The Square and The Triangle. The following year, this was continued with two Ford 16-seaters and two Bedford 27-seaters. No M3 (ERU 403L) was one of the latter. All four were petrol-engined. *S. P. Smith*

Bound for 'the top left hand corner' of the Bournemouth Corporation Transport area — Maclean Road, off Turbany Common — No 114 (DLJ 114L) swings around The Square. The vehicle is a Daimler Fleetline CRL6-30 with 74-seat Alexander bodywork, delivered in 1973. A total of 20 of this type had been received by the following year. The head- and spotlight assemblies had been lowered considerably, compared with earlier models. *Mac Cooper collection*

Continuing the dual-purpose rôle from 1965 were three Leyland Leopard PSU3/2R saloons with 45-seat Weymann bodies. No 101 (CRU 101C), the first of the trio, picks up passengers for Kings Road at Bournemouth Pier whilst upon more prosaic duties. *Carry On* favourite Sid James tops the entertainment at The Pier. Numerous celebrities have participated in publicity stunts for the Transport Department, including Reg Varney from *On the Buses*. *Mac Cooper collection*

Few operators placed repeat orders for Daimler's troubled Roadliner, but Bournemouth came back for a further three in 1968 after an initial batch of eight the previous year. All were Cummins-engined SRC6 models with 49-seat Willowbrook bodywork. No 61 (NRU 61G) was photographed near The Square on 9 February 1969. *M. A. Penn*

Supplied new to Stringer (Prince of Wales Coaches), Amptill, in 1971, passing to Mid-Warwickshire Motors in 1974, this Plaxton Panorama Elite-bodied Leyland Leopard, No 106 (UTM 4K), was one of a pair acquired by Bournemouth in 1976 and used by the Corporation on tour and private hire work alongside native examples delivered new in 1973. It is seen in the town in June 1981. *Kevin Lane*

Smallest of the Department's minibuses were a pair of Ford 12-seaters. No M6 (GEL 224N) was at Holdenhurst Village Green in the winter of 1974/5, on a foray from the Mallard Road depot. The Earl of Malmesbury was the first to ask the Corporation to provide a bus service to Holdenhurst, as early as September 1930. This was in anticipation of that village's being brought into the Borough the following year — and an hourly service was approved in March 1931. *Bournemouth Transport*

Further Leyland Leopard coaches, with Plaxton Supreme IV Express 51-seat bodywork, were purchased in 1979/80. They undertook a wide range of duties, from excursion and private-hire trips to London to rather more workmanlike tasks within Bournemouth itself. On 17 July 1982 No 109 (JLJ 109V) was captured leaving Bournemouth coach station for London Heathrow Airport, whilst on hire to National Express. *G. K. Gillberry*

Two Ford A midibuses with 25-seat Wadham Stringer bodywork were leased in 1979 and numbered in the 'M' series. No M8 is pictured on 7 July 1986, running on a service which was the first motorbus route in the Borough to run at a profit, when from 1923 onwards, the Guy runabouts, and then the Shelvoke & Drewry Tramocars, made it their own. M8 is leaving Boscombe Pier and setting out westbound along Undercliff Drive for Bournemouth Pier. *D. E. Wall*

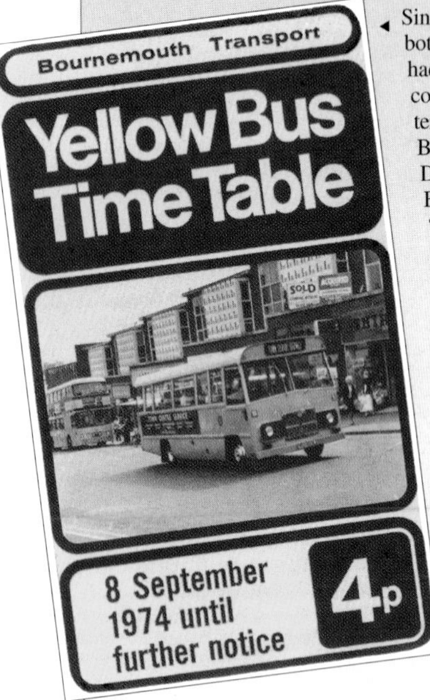

Since before World War 2, both tourists and local people had employed that 'lowest common denominator' terminology beloved of the British, and called Hants & Dorset 'the green buses' and Bournemouth Corporation 'the yellow buses'. This was acknowledged by the Transport Department in the early 'Seventies on the covers of its bus timetable publications. It took a form of marketing agents, however, to suggest that 'Yellow Buses' be used as the fleetname (in 1982). *Colin Morris collection*

Very much of a different feather from the rest of the 'M' series of mini- and midibuses operated in the 'Seventies was No M9 (FEL 209V), a Dodge battery-electric vehicle. It had 18-seat bodywork by Rootes of Maidstone and was purchased in 1979. Its use on the Town Centre Service was largely an extension of the attempt to find a viable way back to electric traction, but, to this day, battery technology is not up to the mark. *D. E. Wall*

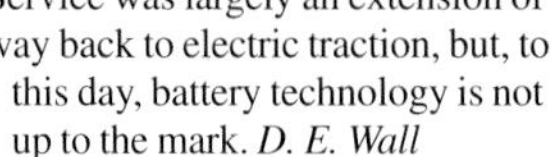

▲ From 1978 onwards several batches of vehicles were acquired on a leasehold basis, including Leyland Fleetlines. No 169 (MFX 169W), an FE30AGR model with 74-seat Alexander bodywork, is pictured at Hants & Dorset's bus station in Poole on 21 April 1981. Route exchanges with the local NBC subsidiary had been introduced in February 1978, bringing service 30 (Poole–Boscombe). No 169 wears the short-lived 'blue flash' logos of the period. *D. E. Wall*

▲ When Bournemouth Transport formally adopted the fleetname 'Yellow Buses/Bournemouth' it engaged in a marketing campaign of (initially) 12 months' duration. Lending his well-known image to the promotion was Bournemouth's own Ken Baily — a local newspaper correspondent, but better known as 'England's No 1 Supporter', whether at Wimbledon, Wembley or covering a streaker's lack of embarrassment with his top hat at Twickenham. Thus, throughout 1982, 'Ken supported the Yellows'. *Ian Allan Library*

▲ Another facet of the promotion involved members of the Bournemouth Symphony Orchestra, pictured here on the top deck of 1978 Leyland Fleetline FE30ALR/ Alexander No 140 (VJT 140S). *Ian Allan Library*

5. Yellow Buses — Bournemouth Transport Ltd

The transport legacy left by Margaret Thatcher's Conservative Government is still the subject of fierce debate. As far as bus services are concerned, however, it is clear that in the early 'Eighties the nationalised and most of the local-authority operators were carrying deficits over to the next financial year. Yellow Buses Bournemouth was numbered among the latter towards the end of the Borough's Works & Transport Committee's direct control.

Part of the radical Transport Act 1985 concerned municipalities which operated their own bus services. It did not state that they should give up such work but rather that municipal transport generally would have to be put 'at arm's length' from its councils. In Bournemouth, the general view of the Works & Transport Committee members was 'why do we have to do this?', and even some of the (then) majority Conservative members wanted to know why it was necessary.

The biggest debate in Council was whether property and land should also be transferred to the new limited-liability company it learned it should now set up. It wanted to retain the depot, in particular, and rent it to the company, but the Government insisted that the Council was obliged to transfer title to the new organisation, together with all the assets.

Bournemouth Transport Ltd began to function on 26 October 1986. It paid for its assets either by shares or loans, so that it remained wholly owned by Bournemouth Council. The board comprised 10 directors, originally under the chairmanship of the leader of the Conservative group. This arrangement continued until 1990, when the Liberal Democrats took a minority hold upon the Council and decided that there should be a non-executive (independent) chairman.

Each member of the board thought: 'Well, this will operate for two or three years and then we'll be told to sell it off' . . . but it didn't happen. Whereas most municipalities divested themselves of their transport departments (including Bournemouth's big neighbours to the east, Southampton and Portsmouth), Bournemouth continues to retain this 'arm's length' control. Why? Councillor Ben Grower: 'I don't think Bournemouth has ever been a great priority for any Government, but at the time they were both very safe Tory seats and I don't believe it was very high up on their agenda.' Ian Cunningham, who became Managing Director of the new company, suggests that one of the reasons was that the department 'had been operating independently of the Council all its life. One of the earliest things the Council said to me when I became Transport Manager in 1964 was "We don't expect you to make a profit; we don't want you to make a loss. Your job is to run the best service that you can from the money you can get from fares, or otherwise, because you're

◂ One of only four of its type built, M10 (HKX 553V), a Bedford JJL with 24-seat Marshall body, was acquired in 1983 from Rambler Coaches of St Leonards-on-Sea, having previously been in the fleet of Maidstone Borough Council. It was recorded at the Bournemouth Pier terminus of the Promenade service to Boscombe Pier on the evening of Monday 2 July 1984. *M. F. Haddon*

Delivered early in 1982, No 195 (TJT 195X) was one of the last new buses to receive 'blue flash' logos; later that year these were replaced with 'Yellow Buses' fleetnames (initially in brown) and the panel at the front — bearing the same legend — was bolted over part of the radiator grille. The bus is a Leyland Olympian ONLXB/1R with 78-seat bodywork by Marshall, one of a batch of 20, which were the last of a long line of Leyland double-deckers delivered to the Department. Looming up from the Lower Pleasure Gardens is a huge tethered balloon used for sightseeing. *D. E. Wall*

never going to get any money from us" . . . Now, I always took the view that if your parameters were clear, that was fine . . . so it made it easier for them to hold on to their transport system.'

There was thus no significant change to the way management had worked before. Its members still had to operate within the budget which they could achieve themselves. They took over the 386 members of staff from the Transport Department, the fleet of 122 double-decker buses, 11 single-deck and five double-deck coaches and four midibuses, and all the necessary items required to keep the services running. As far as the passengers were concerned, there was very little outward difference. The titles 'Yellow Buses' and 'Yellow Coaches' continued in use, and the vehicles turned up on schedule as usual.

From Day One of its existence, Bournemouth Transport Ltd found itself under threat. Before Shamrock & Rambler (a long-established coaching name locally) began stage-carriage operations in the town, using its subsidiary's fleetname 'Charlie's Cars', its representative arrived at Mallard Road: 'We don't want to get into conflict with you; our intention is to work routes that you don't operate on'. However, Shamrock & Rambler quickly discovered that Bournemouth Transport didn't run upon those because there was little money to be made doing so. 'Charlie's Cars' therefore started to encroach upon existing Yellow Buses routes and BT Ltd was forced to engage in the competition envisaged by those in Government who drew up the 1985 legislation. 'Deregulation Day', as 26 October 1986 came to be known in the industry, had also ushered in the new world of competition.

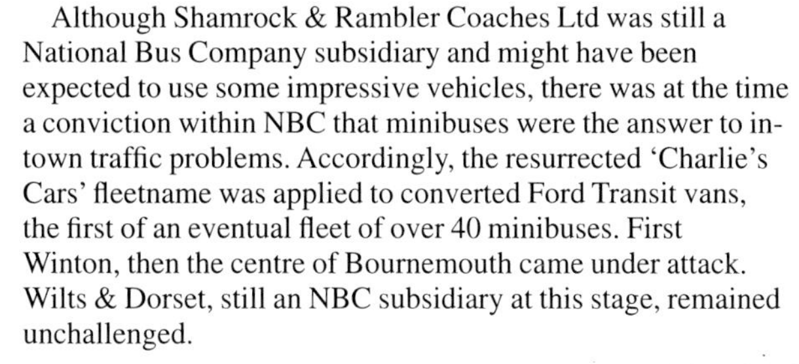

Although Shamrock & Rambler Coaches Ltd was still a National Bus Company subsidiary and might have been expected to use some impressive vehicles, there was at the time a conviction within NBC that minibuses were the answer to in-town traffic problems. Accordingly, the resurrected 'Charlie's Cars' fleetname was applied to converted Ford Transit vans, the first of an eventual fleet of over 40 minibuses. First Winton, then the centre of Bournemouth came under attack. Wilts & Dorset, still an NBC subsidiary at this stage, remained unchallenged.

One of the Olympians (No 183) was converted to double-deck coach configuration and became part of the 'Yellow Coaches' subsidiary arm of the Transport Department. It joined forces with four Leyland Tiger coaches introduced in 1984/5 and bearing this new title in brown, with flashes to match. No 94 (KGS 490Y) was a 50-seat Plaxton-bodied example purchased second-hand in 1984 when one year old. It is departing from Victoria Coach Station, on hire to Shamrock & Rambler, with a picturesque reflection in the windscreen. *Mac Cooper collection*

Wearing two-tone brown flashes and 'Yellow Coaches' fleetnames to match is Leyland Tiger No 96 (B96 TLJ) with Plaxton Paramount 51-seat bodywork — one of a pair delivered in 1985. The vehicle is on a local private-hire assignment, although it was equally likely to be called upon to undertake half- or full-day excursions, long-distance tours in Britain or to cross by ferry to the Continent of Europe. It was in every way a match for any of the coaches on offer from the established tour operators. *Mac Cooper*

Following the Transport Act 1985, municipalities with transport departments were obliged to operate them 'at arm's length' by forming council-controlled limited-liability companies. The last five vehicles ordered by the Transport Department were double-deckers for the continuing 'Yellow Coaches' fleet — Volvo Citybus B10M-50 models with East Lancs 76-seat bodywork. No 202 (D202 ELJ) stands at Bournemouth Pier on the Three Towns Circular.
D. E. Wall

Bournemouth Transport's strategy was primarily to hold on to its existing traffic where possible. The public tended to remain loyal, principally because 7ft 6in-wide minibuses were considered uncomfortable in terms of seating, whereas Yellow Buses continued to employ full-size vehicles with comparatively comfortable and generous seat spacing.

Badgerline's intrusion into the Poole/Bournemouth/Christchurch area, which occurred in the midst of the competition with Shamrock & Rambler, was a rather different story. A representative of Badgerline Group (the privatised extract of the once mighty Bristol Omnibus Co), which had joined forces with the Isle of Wight-based firm Southern Vectis to form 'Badger-Vectis' for this enterprise, made a similar visit to Mallard Road. This time, the assurance was: 'We don't want to operate against you, but against Wilts & Dorset — so, what are the chances of our putting vehicles in your premises and your maintaining them for us?' The BT directors pondered this request. If they were successful against Wilts & Dorset, would they turn their attention upon Yellow Buses? Ian Cunningham was of the opinion that at least an eye could be kept upon them if they were based in Mallard Road, whereas, if they started up somewhere else, they could do whatever they liked.

◄ Competition from newcomers to stage-carriage work, which hit established operators nationwide, came, of course, to Bournemouth following the implementation of the 1985 Act. Shamrock & Rambler was quick to enter the field, using the familiar local fleetname 'Charlie's Cars' for its minibus fleet from October 1986, and 'S &R' on conventional buses from 1988. The following month, Bournemouth countered with second-hand Leyland Nationals, like No 82 (KBB 522L). *Mac Cooper collection*

Thus it was that Badger-Vectis paid BT garage rent and maintenance fees, and signed an agreement that it would give two months' notice of any service change which would affect Yellow Buses. In return, Ian Cunningham was obliged to give it but one month's notice to quit the premises. The seven-month foray of Badger-Vectis began on 6 September 1987. Wilts & Dorset, meanwhile, was not pleased.

The battle with Shamrock & Rambler took a new turn in July 1987, when NBC sold that company to Drawlane Ltd, a subsidiary of Endless Holdings of Salisbury. Although new routes from The Triangle (and in-town adjustments) were introduced by Shamrock & Rambler, it was now free to take on an already embattled Wilts & Dorset, which it started to do on 19 October 1987 — ranging east to west across that firm's coastal area with full-size vehicles. Despite its use of 10 Leyland National saloons run under the 'S&R Buses' identity, and Bournemouth's decision to buy some second-hand examples to combat them, Drawlane's partially-diverted effort marked a turning point for BT in this particular competition. Wilts & Dorset had also responded strongly, and Shamrock & Rambler ceased all stage-carriage activity with effect from 3 December 1988. Some of its 'Charlie's Cars' drivers were taken on by BT to drive its own fleet of hired 'Yellow Flyers' minibuses which had been acquired to take over some of its routes.

The Badger-Vectis story had already come to a conclusion, Wilts & Dorset having defeated the best efforts of that competitor also. In March 1988 Badger-Vectis had begun to threaten Yellow Buses operations, and for a few weeks a bizarre scenario was enacted at Mallard Road depot: Badgerline buses left the garage shadowed by some of those second-hand Leyland Nationals. Bournemouth Transport was housing its own opposition. Then, on 29 March, catching everyone by surprise and without giving statutory notice, Badgerline simply ceased operating and withdrew its vehicles to Bristol and elsewhere. Apart from one or two smaller operators nibbling around the outskirts, BT was able to ease back into its earlier 'understanding' with Wilts & Dorset, and run its services unopposed and more-or-less as it pleased — for a while, at least.

Much of Shamrock & Rambler's 'Charlie's Cars' minibus effort had been based upon the Hampshire Shopping Centre at Strouden Park, and Bournemouth's early response had been to compete strongly with full-size buses. In October 1988 S&R Buses were withdrawn and Bournemouth ran the ex-'Charlie's Cars' routes with eight Freight Rover 'Sherpa' minibuses, ex-Ribble but hired for nine months from Carlyle of Birmingham. With 'Yellow Flyer' arctic-tern logo, No 17 *Chaffinch* (looking more like a canary) exits the Hampshire Centre on 28 January 1989. *D. E. Wall*

In October 1989, Ian Cunningham retired after 25 years at the helm, beating the previous record-holder Ignatius Bulfin by some 18 months. That is a record unlikely to be beaten in Bournemouth, whatever the future holds. He continues to live in the area and, in his mellifluous Edinburgh tones, to call the town 'Bourne Mouth' (the original name of the place) rather than the lazy elision 'Bournemouth' used by the rest of us — still leading by example!

Ted Reid, Deputy Managing Director of Kingston-upon-Hull City Transport Ltd, was appointed to fill the vacancy. Clearly the Council's earlier 'break-even' concept of a successful transport operation had been replaced by something more ambitious. The Board was completely reorganised and Roy Edgley appointed Finance Director

Also set to work on services from the Hampshire Centre were some Mercedes 811D midibuses with Wadham Stringer Wessex bodywork, part of a batch of 20. No 40 (F40 XPR) was the first of these. Here, it is exiting Mallard Road on hire to Hampshire County Council *en route* (HCC's 903) to Lymington, where it participated on a service through the New Forest, taking in Buckler's Hard and Beaulieu, between 21 May and 3 September 1989. Not a lot of people know that! *D. E. Wall*

The 2002 Transport Centenary is Bournemouth's third such municipal event. In 1910 it had a centenary to mark the erection of its first building, and in 1990 had another to celebrate becoming a borough. Suitably painted to mark that event was two-year-old No 205 (E205 GCG), a Volvo Citybus B10M-50 with 80-seat Alexander body. This had been the first new service bus to enter service with Bournemouth Transport Ltd, formed in 1986. *D. E. Wall*

The standard livery for the fleet of Bournemouth Transport Ltd during Ian Cunningham's period as Managing Director remained overall primrose with brown fleetnames. This, then, was the basic livery for a second batch of five Volvo/Alexander 80-seater buses delivered in 1989, bringing the total of this combination to 10. No 213 (F213 WRU), at the Mallard Road depot on 2 July 1989, prepares to go out on service to Alum Chine. *D. E. Wall*

(on 2 January 1990). A fundamental task of Bournemouth Transport Ltd was now to make an annual profit. Accounting and the company's administration were examined in detail. A computer system was introduced: it dealt with the wages from 1 April and all the books by 1 June. Cash-counting and paying-in machines were installed, drivers putting the cash into boxes on wheels rather than lots of bags; the cash office department could now be handled by two people.

The Traffic Department also set up a driver-allocation system, taking several drivers' duties out, without damaging the service to the public. The streamlining of operations and administration turned the business into a profit-making organisation — and every year since has been profitable. Ted Reid started a vehicle-replacement programme in 1990: instead of buying 20 or so buses every two or three years, between four and eight per annum were to be purchased, enabling the fleet to be replaced over a 15- to 18-year cycle. (The exception to this plan would be the Dennis Darts purchased 1995-9 to build up a single-deck fleet.)

Meanwhile, having retired from its brief invasion of the local stage-carriage scene in 1988, Shamrock & Rambler Coaches Ltd

MacVent Ltd, trading as Bournemouth Heritage Transport Services, was formed locally in 1991 and set out to compete with Wilts & Dorset and Bournemouth Transport Ltd, using vehicles initially acquired for preservation. To these it added several ex-London AEC Routemasters. BT retaliated with 'White Buses' — a separate 'W' fleet. No W4 (OEL 124M), a 1974 Daimler Fleetline/Alexander formerly numbered 124, stands at Boscombe in July 1993, on route W2. Overtaking is a competing 'Routemaster Bournemouth' (BHT) bus, also going to The Square. *D. E. Wall*

'Routemaster Bournemouth' also set up shop on the Kinson route (but not in the evenings or at weekends). Bournemouth Transport went one better and purchased five of the larger-capacity ex-London DMS-type Leyland Fleetline, converted to single-door configuration, from Wilts & Dorset. Ready for service W6 to Kinson are Nos W5 (OUC 45R) and W9 (OJD 231R). Both display an advertisement for the swipe-card system which enabled BT to sell 12 journeys for the price of 10, introduced on 'White Buses' but retained after their work was complete. *D. E. Wall*

had concentrated upon its coaching activities, express services to London among them. Unfortunately, this decision coincided with a slump in the popularity of coach tours and excursions nationwide, and the firm simply ceased trading on 29 April 1989 — an event which led to a completely new activity for Bournemouth Transport Ltd. Shamrock & Rambler's latter-day limited-stop London services had been its contribution to the National Express network. The latter plugged this unexpected gap by setting up Dorset Travel Services, of which it owned 50%; the rest was held by three individuals. Dorset Travel Services became tenant at Mallard Road depot, where its coaches in white National Express livery were based and maintained. On 3 April 1992 Bournemouth Transport Ltd purchased Dorset Travel Services and merged it with the Yellow Coaches operation, whose vehicles had been updated regularly in a proportionately similar manner to the buses.

Relative peace at the bus stops had proven somewhat short-lived. Seemingly from nowhere, MacVent Ltd, trading as 'Bournemouth Heritage Transport Services', associated itself with Bournemouth Transport Museum in 1991 and set out to run sightseeing tours with buses previously retired from service. MacVent toyed with the possibility of using the fleetname 'Hants & Dorset' — a notion swiftly dispelled by Wilts & Dorset. Instead, it traded as 'Routemaster Bournemouth' with retired ex-London Transport RMs and local vehicles from the museum, competing strongly on two of Yellow Buses' major routes — 6 (Kinson–The Square) and 20 (Christchurch–The Square). Roy Edgley: 'There were minor variations to it, but in essence it was cherry-picking our two [best] routes, half past eight in the morning until six o'clock at night. It wasn't run in the evenings or at the weekends . . . and quite frequently they missed service . . . it was definitely not genuine competition.'

Bournemouth's response was to set up 'White Buses', with a fleet of a dozen or so second-hand vehicles, and to give more choice to its passengers. The Wayfarer 3 ticketing system was introduced on these buses, together with a swipe-card facility offering 12 journeys for the price of 10. Off-peak tickets and one-week tickets were sold on board — and still are. It worked: in 1995 MacVent, Bournemouth Transport Museum and Bournemouth Transport Ltd held discussions. Vintage Yellow Buses Ltd, with a capital of £100, became a subsidiary of Bournemouth Transport Ltd, with Ted Reid as its Chairman. This retitled company, most of whose vehicles were now owned by BT Ltd, now reverted in its new colours to the running of specified sightseeing routes in the area. Marc Reddy, who had joined Bournemouth Transport from school initially but taken a degree at Plymouth University, had been given the job of running White Buses. He had undertaken the task with great enthusiasm, and it was largely because of his efforts that the competition had been successfully dealt with. He was subsequently made Traffic Manager and, later, Coaching Director.

Primarily to carry out the contract work awarded to BT Ltd, but also to provide a vintage service to various places, together with open-top tours, 'Christchurch Buses' — in an attractive blue and cream livery — emerged from Vintage Yellow Buses, but it was always really a part of Bournemouth Transport Ltd. Its active existence ceased in September 2000, when the vehicles were recalled from Poole (!) to Mallard Road depot.

In 1995 Bournemouth Transport Ltd expanded its National Express work by taking over provision of the latter's Portsmouth–

▲ Vehicles in full Bournemouth Transport livery were also fitted with W-series destination blinds and thrown into the fray against Bournemouth Heritage Transport and its subsequent identities. No 536 (RWA 860R) was one of four examples of the Bristol VR/ECW double-decker — an NBC standard type — purchased second-hand from Yorkshire Traction, and which served in this rôle from January to September 1994, offering half fares for senior citizens on the W routes. *Mac Cooper collection*

London operation, its coaches parked in a yard on Portsea Island (once proud Southdown territory) with just a ticket office and locally-employed drivers. Five Scania K113CRB/Van Hool 49-seater coaches formed the initial fleet allocated, with some 11 vehicles eventually making up this isolated outpost. The main effort, meanwhile, was in erstwhile Royal Blue territory: Weymouth–Poole–Bournemouth–London. In addition, coaches on the Eurolines service from London to Paris (operated from 1993 to date) parked in a small garage nicknamed 'Sammy's' at Victoria Coach Station, so called because it was originally owned by Samuelson's of London. The garage is run by Dorset Travel.

It was Ted Reid who introduced a major revision of the livery carried by the stage-carriage vehicles. Out went the last vestiges of brown, to be replaced by fleetname, skirt and roof painted in blue, representing (from bottom to top) the blue waters of Poole Bay, the yellow sand on the beach, and the blue skies, of which Bournemouth enjoys a generous share. Reid left his mark also upon the social life of the town. He is recalled affectionately as a good stand-up comedian, raconteur and after-dinner speaker in the traditional Lancashire mode. And when, after nearly 10 years in post, he retired in September 1999, it was to Burnley, Lancashire, that he returned.

Roy Edgley was promoted to Managing Director on 1 October 1999, retaining in addition his rôle as Finance Director. He heads a Board of nine members; in addition to an Operations Director and an Engineering Director (who, together with the MD himself, comprise the three executive members), there are three Council directors (representing Labour, Liberal Democrat and Conservative), two non-executive directors (not councillors but businessmen in their own right) and a staff-nominated director.

'Routemaster Bournemouth' was taken over in December 1994. The Board of Directors was subsequently changed — with Ted Reid, Managing Director of Bournemouth Transport Ltd, becoming Chairman — and it was again re-branded, as 'Vintage Yellow Buses'. This firm became a subsidiary of BT and traded in Bournemouth Corporation livery. Most of its vehicles were owned by BT and were 'hired out' to Christchurch Buses, created by to operate contracts and vintage open-top tours. On 25 September 1997, No 111 (DLJ 111L), a 1973 Fleetline in full Christchurch livery, operates a Town Tour. *D. E. Wall*

When Badgerline arrived upon the competitive stage in September 1987, it had its vehicles housed and maintained at BT's Mallard Road depot — having convinced the incumbent that its local intrusion was not aimed at Yellow Buses. A spin-off from this relationship was a one-month hire of a liquid-petroleum-gas-powered Badgerline Bristol VR, BH5508 (KOU 794P), seen at Mallard Road on 22 February 1996. The experiment did not lead to purchase. *Tim Weatherup*

Bournemouth Transport Ltd bought Dorset Travel Services in 1993. The latter had been 50%-owned by National Express, and its white coaches had been tenants at Mallard Road. BT merged its new acquisition with the Yellow Coaches operation but kept over 20 coaches in white 'express' livery and actually expanded this business in 1995 by taking over operation of the Portsmouth–London service, which it ran until September 2001. No 352 (P352 ARU), a Scania K113CRB/Van Hool Alizée HE of 1997 (albeit seen at Poole) represents that six-year outpost. *D. E. Wall*

Ted Reid became Managing Director of Bournemouth Transport Ltd in 1989, following the retirement of long-serving Ian Cunningham. One of Reid's more obvious innovations was a new livery for 'Yellow Buses' — out went the maroon used since 1902, replaced by logos, skirt and roof painted blue, to represent 'the blue sea, the yellow sand and the blue sky'. No 210 (F210 WRU), a 1989 Volvo in the new livery, passes along Glenferness Avenue, watched by transport photographer and author Philip Davies. *Colin Morris*

Bournemouth and that most 'Hampshire' of towns, Christchurch, were transferred into the county of Dorset in 1974. Hampshire County Cricket Club ignored that for many years, and the West Hants Lawn Tennis Club still does. With its overall advertising, 1991 Dennis Dominator No 261 (H261 MFX) seems fully committed to the new authority, but old loyalties lurk in the background: the East Lancs-bodied 80-seater is passing the Boscombe social club of the 7th Battalion, Royal Hampshire Home Guard. *D. E. Wall*

Thus the three executive directors and the two non-executive directors have a majority on the Board, which means that there is no Council directive which necessarily overrides everything else. Yet all the shares are still held by Bournemouth Council, and the nominated shareholder is the Chief Executive of the Council.

The main problem the company faces is the age-old one of a very high summer peak necessitating the operation in winter of more double-deckers than that season demands, such that some vehicles then run fairly empty. Some buses are mothballed at that time, particularly the convertible open-toppers, which are getting old and are used only during the summer. To be precise, the real peak is from the beginning of June to halfway through July, when there are visitors arriving while children are still in school. Once the schools break for the summer holiday, that releases some eight or nine vehicles which help to cover the July and August peak and enable the company to run its open-top coastal service 12. Additional drivers and other staff are taken on in this period.

Where once the trams and then trolleybuses crossed the River Stour, Dennis Dominator DDA1033 No 262 (H262 MFX) has just passed over Tuckton Bridge, going west to Bournemouth Square, on 22 August 1996. It looks good in primrose and blue with a full complement of advertisements — a far cry from April 1934, when a Council sub-committee strongly deprecated the display of advertisements on Hants & Dorset buses, and communicated that view to the company. Bournemouth first allowed external advertising on the buses in 1966, with the first overall advert appearing in 1981.
D. E. Wall

Crossing the Hampshire Avon (now in Dorset) on Waterloo Bridge, Christchurch, comes the first of six Dennis Lance 11SDA saloons delivered in 1993. The engine is a 211bhp Cummins 6CT and the East Lancs bodywork provides 48 seats, with room for 17 standing passengers. The vehicle, ex Bournemouth Square via Boscombe, is approaching its terminus outside the Council offices in Waterloo Place, Christchurch, on a sunny morning in June 2001.
Colin Morris

When suitable smaller-capacity saloon buses were purchased in 1995, it was decided to 'route brand' two services — 'Super-Route 6' from Kinson into town, and 'Super-Route 17' from Throop to Alum Chine via Bournemouth Square. On layover in Avenue Road, Bournemouth, is No 451 (M451 LLJ), a Dennis Dart 9.8SDL, the first of 22 delivered in 1995/6. It has a 130bhp Cummins B-series engine and 40-seat (+16 standees) bodywork by East Lancs. *D. E. Wall*

Delivered in June 1998 and allocated to the branded 'Super-Route 6' service is No 479 (R479 NPR), a 10m Dennis Dart SLF, seen taking a rest from its duties in Bourne Avenue on 26 September 2000. The bodywork is a super-low-floor Spryte model by East Lancs with 37 seats and room for another 18 passengers standing. The engine is the standard 130bhp Cummins B, utilised in both Dennis Dart types employed by BT, the 10m SLF being marginally the heavier. *D. E. Wall*

In the year 2000 the company expanded its day-tour business by purchasing a local small business owned by the Brough family — Whippet Coaches — with five coaches and three minibuses, which are now based at Mallard Road. The DAF/Ikarus 49-seater is operated with 'Grand UK' logos, but the remainder retain their white Whippet livery, with just the legal ownership address block to identify their connection with Yellow Coaches. In addition, Yellow Coaches has two of its vehicles in Leger Holidays livery. On the other hand, some difficulties were encountered with the company's contribution to the National Express service from Portsmouth, in particular the need for a company official to go there to interview new drivers aboard a coach — there being no office locally — or summon them to Bournemouth. Accordingly, this operation was relinquished in September 2001, which reduced the coach fleet to 34 vehicles.

In 2001, for the first time ever, the staff were invited to help select the company's next intake of vehicles. Members of the Engineering Department as a whole selected Volvo as the successful competitor for the delivery of eight super-low-floor chassis. The drivers were asked to consider the design of the driving seat (neck and back movements being taken into account), and an innovative high-backed model was chosen. For the East Lancs bodywork, passengers were asked which type of seat they preferred, and discussion led to the choice of a 'safer' straight staircase to the upper deck. The result was a strong

Captain and Mrs Norton's cupola and clock survive atop a new building in The Square on 12 July 2000, as two Dennis Trident super-low-floor double-deckers of 1999 share Gervis Place with a 'Super-Route 6' Dennis Dart. The former are Nos 270 (T270 BPR) and 273 (T273 BPR) with East Lancs 84-seat bodywork and Cummins 6CT engines — representative of a batch of nine — travelling to Bear Wood via Winton, and Bear Cross via Wallisdown, respectively. *D. E. Wall*

and sturdy, highly-functional yet striking vehicle. As an interesting contrast with those very early motorbus prices, each cost somewhere in the region of £145,000.

For the express-service fleet, the company buys to National Express standard, currently Volvo/ or Scania/Van Hool, whereas Volvo/Berkhof is the vehicle of the moment for Yellow Coaches, of which Dorset Travel Services Ltd became a dormant subsidiary in March 2001.

All the management team of Bournemouth Transport Ltd live in the town, and consider that they are members of a community business, providing both a social and a financial dividend — and helping numerous local charities along the way. And now, at a time when Bournemouth Transport is celebrating its centenary, Councillor Ben Grower sums up: 'The people of Bournemouth know it's owned by the Council; they know it's their bus company. They identify "Yellow Buses" with Bournemouth. It's an efficient, good-looking fleet by any standard — and that's got to do with the good professionals we have there managing it. Although I was very much against the setting up of the company originally, I now think it's a good way of running local transport, provided some regulation is built in, so that we are guaranteed to remain in existence.'

The future of the undertaking may well depend upon the balance of power in Council. More Glory Days? There's always hope.

David Chalk joined Bournemouth Corporation Transport at the age of 16 years, rising to the rank of Traffic Superintendent and, finally, Coaching Manager. In addition, he compiled every celebratory booklet produced by the Department. A great surprise awaited him upon his retirement in 2000. The Mayor, Cllr Jim Courtney, led him to the front of No 334 (W334 UEL), a Volvo B10M-62/Berkhof Axial 50. Magically, it had become *The David Chalk*. *D. E. Wall*

Service A1 (The Square–Bournemouth International Airport) is provided primarily for Ryanair passengers on the Dublin service. On 12 July 2001 driver Malcolm Weinberg changes the screen as his customers join those boarding Boeing 737 EI-CNY bound for Ireland. No 315 (X315 WFX) is a Mercedes 614D with 24-seat Crest Coach Conversion body; it was delivered to Bournemouth Transport Ltd in September 2000 bearing Dorset Travel Services fleetnames.
Colin Morris

Bournemouth International Airport at Hurn is now owned by Manchester Airport plc and has runways long enough to cope with a Concorde or Boeing 747. As part of its contract with the Irish airline Ryanair, however, it is obliged to provide a bus service. That is run on contract by Bournemouth Transport's Yellow Coaches subsidiary. On the airport forecourt is the one-off Mercedes 614D midibus purchased specially for this service. *Colin Morris*

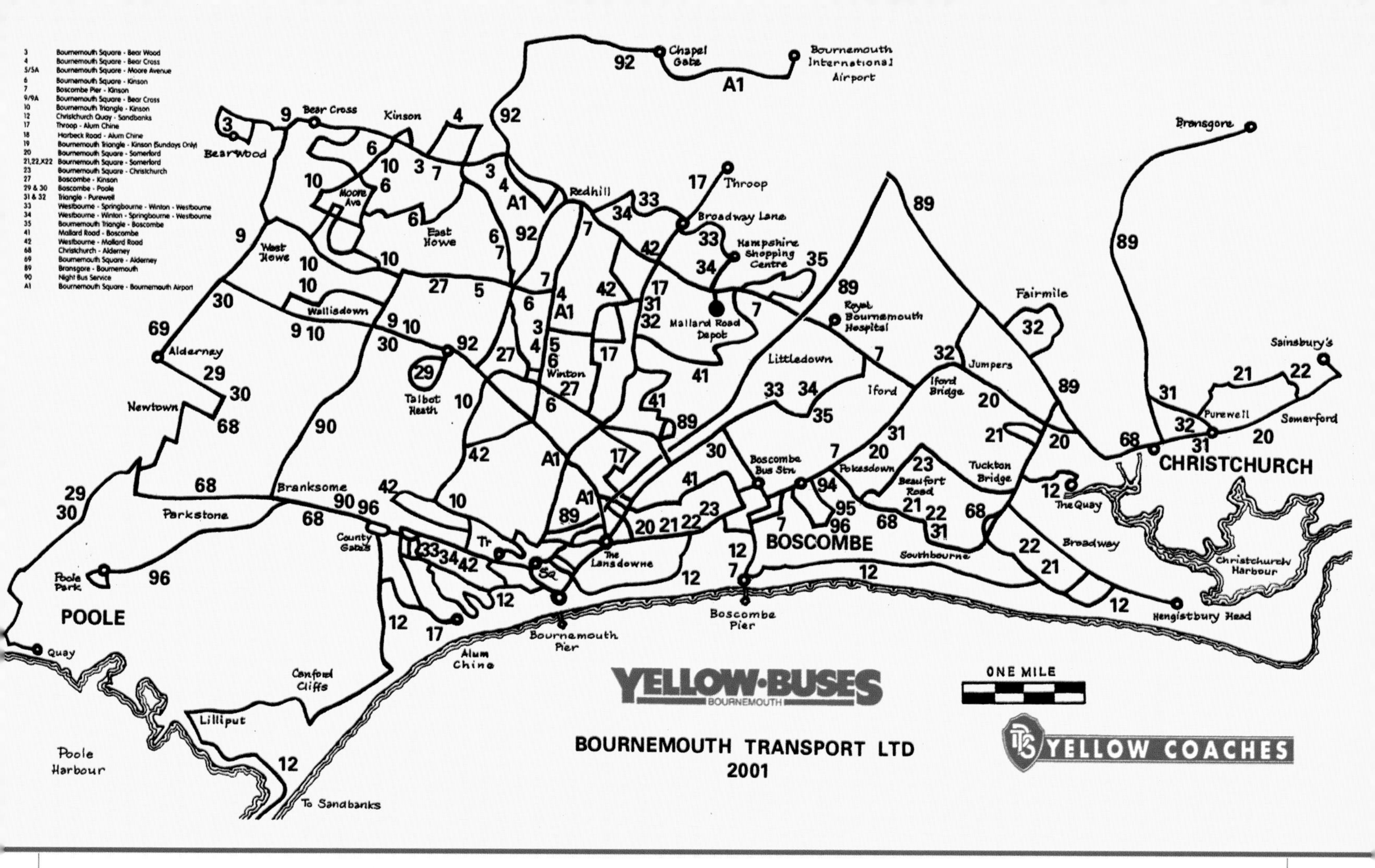

Yellow Buses route map, 2001. Routes to Poole, once served by Bournemouth's trams but not its trolleybuses, were restored in a somewhat roundabout fashion by Bournemouth Transport buses in 1978. At the same time, open-top double-deckers on the summer coastal service extended their route to Sandbanks, previously served by Hants & Dorset buses. This followed that firm's disastrous 1976 fire at its famous bus station, and the temporary housing of its local buses at Mallard Road. Since then there have been extensions to the north and east and considerable in-filling of routes. The route to Bournemouth Airport is nominally a Yellow Coaches operation. *Colin Morris*

Crossing the Hampshire Avon between Bridge Street and Castle Street, Christchurch, is the first of eight super-low-floor Volvo B7TL/East Lancs Vyking double-deckers delivered in April and May 2001. It has bodywork with 76 seats and room for 14 standing passengers, a Volvo D7C engine and high-ratio differential equipment. On 12 June 2001 Cllr Ben Grower — a Yellow Buses director — emerged from his premises and observed with justifiable pride: 'Here comes one of our new Volvos — just look at that!' *Colin Morris*

Further Reading

Among the books I have found helpful and/or recommend for further reading are:

Anderson, R. C. *The History of the Tramways of Bournemouth & Poole*, Light Railway Transport League, 1964.

Anderson, Roy C. *Bournemouth and Poole Tramways*, Middleton Press, Midhurst, 2001.

Bowler, D. *Bournemouth Trolleybuses*, JTPP, 2001.

Chalk, David L. *Bournemouth Trolleybuses*, Official Souvenir, Bournemouth Corporation Transport, 1969.

Chalk, David L. *Bournemouth Transport: 75 Years*, Souvenir Brochure, BCT, 1977.

Chalk, David L. *Yellow Buses: Bournemouth 85th Anniversary*, Bournemouth Transport Ltd, 1987.

Chalk, David L. *Bournemouth Transport Centenary*, Brochure, 2002.

Klapper, Charles *The Golden Age of Tramways*, David & Charles, Newton Abbot, 1961.

Mawson, J. *Bournemouth Corporation Transport*, Advertiser Press Ltd, Huddersfield, 1967.

Morris, Colin *Hants & Dorset — a history*, DTS Publishing Ltd, Croydon, 1996.

Owen, Nicholas *History of the British Trolleybus*, David & Charles, Newton Abbot, 1974.

Robert, C. G., & Jackson, B. L. *Trams and Buses of Poole*, The Oakwood Press, Usk, 2001.

Also numerous articles over the years in *Buses Illustrated* and *Buses*, journals published by Ian Allan Ltd.